Ma

DIRECTIONS

WRITTEN AND RESEARCHED BY

Matthew Hancock

WITH ADDITIONAL ACCOUNTS BY

Amanda Tomlin and Jane Gordon

ROUGH
GUIDES

NEW YORK • LONDON • DELHI

www.roughguides.com

Contents

Introduction to

Madeira

Surrounded by the warm seas of the Atlantic some 600km off the west coast of Morocco, Madeira is an island of wild mountains, precipitous valleys and sheer cliffs – including the second-highest sea cliffs in the world at Cabo Girão. The island's dramatic scenery makes for some fantastic walking, and it also boasts a diverse array of colourful semi-tropical vegetation, gently cultivated terraces and rocky beaches. Its lesser-known sister island, Porto Santo, may not possess such an exciting landscape, but it does have a superb nine-kilometre-long beach.

The island's year-round mild climate, excellent hotel facilities, splendid botanical gardens and extremely low levels of crime have long attracted older visitors, though these days a much younger crowd is being lured by the excellent *levada* walks (along a network of irrigation canals) and the growing number of sports on offer, such as golf, deep-sea fishing, diving and surfing.

When to go

Semi-permanent sunshine makes Madeira an all-year destination. Northern Europeans visit mostly in winter, when average maximum daily temperatures are around 20°C. Portuguese visitors predominate in summer (around 24°C). Peak time, however, is undoubtedly over New Year, when hotels hike up their prices by some thirty percent. Other busy times coincide with school holidays, so low season, such as it is, tends to be late October to early December and late January to March, which also coincides with the wettest months. Outside high summer, rain is possible at any time, though it rarely sets in for long.

Porto Santo has its own climate. Rainfall is very low and most days are dry and sunny, though it can be breezy. Low cloud, known as *capacete*, sometimes descends from the mountains at around lunchtime, though this usually clears by mid-afternoon and acts as a handy shield against the strongest sun of the day.

▲ On the trail from Pico do Arieiro to Pico Ruivo

Madeira and Porto Santo were uninhabited until they were discovered and colonized by Portuguese explorers in the fifteenth century. Thanks to its strategic position on a major shipping route, Madeira soon established itself as an important trading post, linking Portugal with its colonies in Africa and America. In the seventeenth century, the British – Portugal's traditional commercial ally – largely took control of a burgeoning wine trade, leading to a stong British influence on the island's elite. Influential Anglo–Madeiran familes can be found to this day, but, although English is widely spoken, the population is nearly all of mainland Portuguese descent – the signs, culture and architecture are Portuguese, and so are the superb pastries, powerful coffees and top table wines.

▶ Câmara de Lobos

▲ A Funchal doorway

Once one of the poorest parts of Portugal and consequently of Europe, Madeira gained semi-autonomous status within the Portuguese Republic in 1976 and the island has since flourished. Its president has successfully lobbied for EU funds to subsidize new roads, tunnels and building projects that have propelled most of the island firmly into the twenty-first century. These days Madeirans are not only proudly Portuguese, but proudly Madeiran too.

Madeira's building boom continues, but equal efforts have been made to preserve its natural heritage: the island boasts the greatest concentration of virgin lauraceous forests in the world, and an astonishing 66 percent of the island enjoys protected national-park status. Despite its compact size, there are parts of the island where you feel as though you're in the middle of a magical wilderness.

▲ Mercado dos Lavradores, Funchal

Madeira
AT A GLANCE

Funchal

Funchal is the island's historic capital. Very Portuguese in character and architecture, the town has enough museums, sights, restaurants, bars and shops to keep you occupied for at least a week. It is also close to many of the island's top tourist attractions, including Monte, a pretty hilltop town famed for its gardens and dry toboggan run, and Câmara de Lobos, an atmospheric fishing village that Winston Churchill took to his heart.

▲ The mountainous interior

Western Madeira

Ribeira Brava, set among verdant banana plantations, is the only place approaching resort status along the unspoilt western coastline. That may change, as Jardim do Mar and Paúl do Mar have a growing surf culture, while Calheta can boast an artificial sandy beach and a brand-new marina. Inland there are superb walks around the wooded valleys of Rabaçal.

◄ Café do Museu, Funchal

Eastern Madeira

Relatively built up, eastern Madeira's highlights include Machico, the island's first capital; the rocky peninsula of Ponta de São Lourenço, with Madeira's only natural sand beach; and Santo da Serra, home to the island's top golf course. The main resort is Caniço de Baixo, with superb swimming and diving possibilities.

▲ Levada da Central de Janela

▲ Pico do Arieiro

Northwestern Madeira

The northwest of the island is wild and dramatic, with precipitous hillsides gouged by waterfalls spilling down to the Atlantic. The main centres here are Porto Moniz, which has invigorating natural sea pools, and São Vicente, one of the island's prettiest villages, close to some weird volcanic grottoes.

Northeastern Madeira

Highlights in the northeast include Santana, famed for its triangular houses, and the picturesque village of Porto da Cruz. Also in this area, the dramatic peaks of Pico Arieiro and Pico Ruivo, more than 1800m high, offer great walks and fantastic Alpine-like views over the island's coasts.

Porto Santo

Easily accessible by ferry or plane, Porto Santo, Madeira's neighbouring island, boasts a sumptuous sandy beach and the pretty town of Vila Baleira.

▲ Porto Santo's beach

Ideas

The big six

Madeira's main sights are readily accessible from any point of the island and can easily be visited during a week's stay. The following give an idea of the diverse attractions available, from historic towns and churches to natural wonders such as towering mountains and sheer cliff faces, not to mention the superb sandy beach on the neighbouring island of Porto Santo.

▲ Funchal

The only town of any size on Madeira, the attractive capital makes the perfect base for exploring the island.

P.51 ▸ Central Funchal

▲ Monte

A hilltop town boasting great views, lush gardens and the island's most sacred church, guarding a venerated statue of the Virgin.

P.93 ▸ Monte and northeast of Funchal

▶ Pico Ruivo

At 1862m high, this accessible mountain peak offers stupendous views – they're still pretty impressive even when the valley below is shrouded in clouds, as it often is.

P.171 ▶ Northern and central Madeira

◀ Porto Santo

Perhaps Europe's best-kept secret, Madeira's sister island has 9km of pristine sands.

P.178 ▶ Porto Santo

▶ Machico

With its own little beach and surrounded by banana plantations, this historic town makes a great alternative base to Funchal.

P.118 ▶ South-eastern Madeira

◀ Cabo Girão

Whether viewed from the sea or from the top, the world's second-highest sea cliffs are a spectacular sight.

P.107 ▶ Northwest of Funchal

Walks

Madeira is rightly famous for its walks. Many of these are along well-marked *veredas* (paths), used by locals to travel from village to village before the road network was constructed. Even more popular are the *levada* walks, along the sides of irrigation canals that wend through some of the island's wildest scenery. The *levadas* cover some 2000km; make sure you're well prepared and follow local advice, as some pass through tunnels and across precipitous terrain.

CALDEIRÃO
ERDE 6,5 KM

LDEIRÃO DO
ERNO 8 KM

▼ Lorano to Machico

An exhilarating clifftop path high above the north coast.

P.133 ▶ Northeastern Madeira

▼ Prazeres to Paúl do Mar

Zigzag down one of the west coast's steepest cliffs, with great views en route.

P.144 ▶ The west

▼ Pico do Arieiro to Pico Ruivo

Madeira's most famous and memorable route, between two of its highest peaks.

P.173 ▸ Northern and central Madeira

▲ Rabaçal to 25 Fontes

A beautiful *levada* walk deep into lush woodland.

P.146 ▸ The west

◀ Levada do Caldeirão Verde

One of the island's most spectacular *levada* walks winds through ancient laurel forests.

P.170 ▸ Northern and central Madeira

▶ Levada da Central da Janela, Porto Moniz

An attractive, gentle *levada* hike that takes you into the heart of the rural north.

P.157 ▸ Porto Moniz and the northwest

Transport

Getting around Madeira, surrounded by the Atlantic, fringed by cliffs and rising inland to 1862m above sea level, has long posed problems to voyagers and engineers alike. Over time, many of the island's most challenging features have been ingeniously exploited to provide easy access and highly enjoyable ways of getting from A to B. From dry toboggans to high-tech lifts and cable cars, many of the rides are worth going on for the thrill alone.

▲ Lift to Fajã das Padres

The beachside settlement of Fajã das Padres is reached by a thrilling descent down the cliff face in a glass-fronted lift.

P.109 ▸ Northwest of Funchal

▼ Santa Maria de Columbo

Get a different perspective on the island on a boat trip from Funchal harbour.

P.199 ▶ Essentials

▼ Cable car at Santana

Not for the faint-hearted, this dizzy descent is an adrenalin-pumping way to see the wild north coast.

P.168 ▶ Northern and central Madeira

▲ Cable car to Monte

The best views over Funchal are from the slowly ascending cable car from the Zona Velha.

P.86 ▶ Eastern Funchal and the Old Town

▲ Monte toboggan

Traditional basket toboggans are a bizarre, novel and undoubtedly exhilarating way to get down a mountain.

P.97 ▶ Monte and northeast of Funchal

Sports and activities

The opening of Porto Santo's golf course means there are now three top golf courses in this corner of the Atlantic. Madeira's climate and terrain are also ideal for several other sports: game fishing is big business, surfing has a dedicated following and an increasing number of companies offer adventure sports, from canyoning to diving. Madeira's national sport, however, is football, and the island that produced the silky skills of Cristiano Ronaldo also has teams in Portugal's top division.

▲ Porto Santo Golf

Porto Santo Golf, in the heart of Madeira's sister island, is rated the best course in the area.

P.184 ▸ Porto Santo

▲ Diving

Explore sea caverns, wrecks and the clear, deep water, swimming with moray eels, Atlantic rays and mantas.

P.199 ▸ Essentials

▼ Mountain bikes

Get off the beaten track on a mountain-bike trip along the spectacular *levada* paths.

P.199 ▶ Essentials

▲ Fishing

The deep waters around Madeira offer some of the best big game fishing in the world; take a fishing trip from Funchal harbour.

P.199 ▶ Essentials

▲ Surfing

Madeira has a burgeoning reputation as a surfing centre, and one of the top places to take to the waves is Jardim do Mar.

P.199 ▶ Essentials

▼ Marítimo

Catch one of Portugal's top teams, Marítimo, who entertain the likes of Porto and Benfica.

P.200 ▶ Essentials

Picnic spots

Tropical fruits and fresh produce are relatively inexpensive at Madeira's vibrant markets, the best places to stock up on food and drink for a picnic. Madeirans love nothing better than taking off for a summer picnic, and there are little wooden benches dotted round the island's most scenic spots. In the mountains you'll also find brick or stone barbecues.

▲ Portela

Find a spot near the stalls selling bulbs at this dramatic mountain pass offering a sweeping panorama of the north coast.

P.132 ▶ Northeastern Madeira

▼ Queimadas

Little Red Riding Hood wouldn't look out of place in the fairy-tale scenery of this UNESCO-protected forest.

P.169 ▸ Northern and central Madeira

▼ Ribeiro Frio

Tree ferns and exotic vegetation high in the mountains provide a pleasant shady spot for a picnic.

P.172 ▸ Northern and central Madeira

▲ Ponta do Pargo

Perch on the clifftop at the westernmost point in Madeira.

P.152 ▸ Porto Moniz and the north-west

▲ Baia de Abra

Enjoy views of Ponta de São Lourenço at this breezy bluff, and watch out for lizards, who may take a fancy to your picnic.

P.129 ▸ Northeastern Madeira

Swimming

It's commonly assumed that Madeira has few beaches, but in fact nearly every coastal village has some sort of beach or jetty that you can swim off. There are fifteen Blue Flag beaches in total, and though most of these consist of large stones, two have soft sand. Many places also have a *complexo balnear* or lido, coastal sea pools, usually supervised in summer. And virtually every hotel of three stars and above has its own pool.

▲ Porto Santo

The island's southeast coast is one long expanse of superb sand, perfect for families.

P.178 ▸ Porto Santo

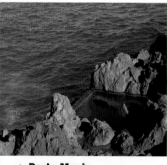

▲ Porto Moniz

This north-coast village is famed for its natural sea pools, hollowed out from the volcanic rock.

P.154 ▸ Porto Moniz and the northwest

▼ Prainha

Madeira's only natural sandy beach, a popular stretch of soft black sand.

P.128 ▶ Northeastern Madeira

▲ Ponta Delgada

Lovely fresh water and a poolside café-bar make this lido the summer hub of the village.

P.163 ▶ Northern and central Madeira

▼ Porto da Cruz

Safe bathing with a breathtaking backdrop of towering mountains.

P.132 ▶ Northeastern Madeira

▲ Foz da Ribeira

Sea pools in an idyllic river valley on the dramatic north coast.

P.167 ▶ Northern and central Madeira

Parks and gardens

Madeira means "wood" and was so named because of its lauraceous forests, one of the earth's last great concentrations of laurel trees – in 1999 they were declared a UNESCO world heritage site. The island's climate also supports a wide range of the world's most beautiful cultivated flora, many introduced from ships calling in on their way back from South Africa, Australasia, Asia and South America. As a result, many parks and gardens have exotic plants bursting into bloom virtually year round.

▲ Jardim Botânico, Funchal

Funchal's botanical gardens offer a diverse range of stunning flora, from palms to exotic cacti and bird-of-paradise plants.

P.87 ▶ Eastern Funchal and the Old Town

▼ Jardins Tropicais do Monte

A park-cum-museum, boasting works of art, decorative tiles, koi carp and abundant tropical vegetation.

P.96 ▶ Monte and northeast of Funchal

▼ Palheiro Gardens

Elaborate formal gardens that show off Madeira's prolific plant life.

P.100 ▶ Monte and northeast of Funchal

▲ Jardim de Santa Catarina

A highly scenic and popular town park, complete with a lake and fine views.

P.69 ▶ Western Funchal and the Hotel Zone

▲ Rosarium, Arco de São Jorge

Portugal's largest rose collection, with over one thousand species.

P.166 ▶ Northern and central Madeira

Museums

In its heyday, Madeira was a glorified service station on the shipping highways between Europe, Africa, South America and Asia. Christopher Columbus set up here, keen to exploit the island's rich commercial potential, as did the Flemish, who traded works of art for sugar. This exchange has left a rich legacy of artefacts and paintings that can be enjoyed in Madeira's museums. You can also find out about more recent influences on island life, such as whaling.

▲ Museu de Arte Sacra

Set in a former Bishop's Palace, the Renaissance Flemish paintings here are testament to Madeira's once-powerful trading status.

P.58 ▸ Central Funchal

▲ Museu da Baleia, Caniçal

An engaging museum, recording the history of the island's whaling industry.

P.128 ▸ Northeast Madeira

▼ Museu Fotografia Vicentes

An evocative collection of black-and-white photos of nineteenth- and twentieth-century Madeira.

P.59 ▶ Central Funchal

▲ Casa Museu Cristovão Colombo

The great explorer's heavily restored Porto Santo home, full of fascinating memorabilia.

P.181 ▶ Porto Santo

◀ Palácio de São Lourenço

Funchal's most impressive historic building, a series of magnificent state rooms stuffed with works of art.

P.54 ▶ Central Funchal

▶ Fortaleza de São Tiago

The capital's seventeenth-century fortress, where you can visit an eclectic collection of modern art and then clamber round the ramparts.

P.86 ▶ Eastern Funchal and the Old Town

Azulejos

Madeira has some fine examples of *azulejos*, the distinctive Portuguese glazed tiles, used to decorate everything from the exterior of houses, walls and fountains to the interiors of churches and cafés. The craft was brought to Portugal by the Moors in the eighth century – the word "*azulejo*" derives from the Arabic *al-zulecha*, "small stone". Useful both for insulation and decoration, tiles continue to be used on buildings to this day, though most are now factory-produced imitations of the old hand-painted forms.

▲ Quinta Vigia

Azulejos depicting the life of Saint Francis embellish the chapel of the president's house.

P.70 ▸ Western Funchal and the Hotel Zone

▼ Jardins Tropicais do Monte Palace

These modern *azulejos* illustrate key moments in Portuguese history.

P.96 ▶ Northeast of Funchal

▲ Casa dos Azulejos

Fine Portuguese tiles alongside those from Turkey, Syria and elsewhere.

P.61 ▶ Central Funchal

▼ Praça do Município

The former Chamber of Commerce on Avenida Arriaga is typical of some of central Funchal's elaborately decorated older buildings.

P.58 ▶ Central Funchal

▲ Convento de Santa Clara

The seventeenth-century tiles in this convent are some of the oldest on the island.

P.61 ▶ Central Funchal

Festivals

Usually coinciding with local saints' days or harvests, Madeira's festivals are occasions for the locals to let rip, and they follow a similar format: religious services in the church followed by folk dancing, usually accompanied by live music. Food stalls, lots of alcohol and sometimes fireworks enliven the proceedings. The main festivals have become more commercial, with the biggest ones – at New Year and for carnival – becoming tourist attractions in their own right.

▲ Madeira Wine Festival

Kick off your shoes and join in the grape-treading with the locals.

P.202 ▸ Essentials

▲ Vintage Car Rally

The annual touring of hardy relics dating back to the 1920s.

P.201 ▸ Essentials

▲ New Year's Eve fireworks

Let the new year in with a bang: some of the finest fireworks you'll ever see.

P.201 ▸ Essentials

▼ Funchal Carnival

The closest Europe has to a Rio-style parade, both literally and figuratively.

P.201 ▸ Essentials and
p.60 ▸ Central Funchal

▲ Festa da Flor

A three-day flower festival turns central Funchal into a riot of colour.

P.201 ▸ Essentials

▼ Columbus week

Porto Santo's Columbus week celebrations involve a replica sixteenth-century sailing boat and a mock wedding.

P.202 ▸ Essentials

Children's Madeira

With its stony beaches and traditionally older visitors, Madeira has a somewhat unjustified reputation for not being suitable for children. Certainly, if your children are only happy with buckets and spades on a big sandy beach, then Porto Santo is a better option. However, for older children who enjoy outdoor activities, there's no shortage of things to do at any time of the year. As on mainland Portugal, children are welcomed everywhere and, while you're unlikely to find specific facilities such as baby-changing areas, the locals will do their best to accommodate children's requirements.

▲ **Jungle Rain café**

A remote but hugely popular family restaurant, complete with jungle noises and stuffed animals.

P.151 ▶ The west

▲ **Beatles Boat**

Even the most restless children enjoy dining on these fixed boats, surrounded by fish.

P.54 ▶ Central Funchal

▼ Horse rides, Porto Santo

Take a traditional *carriola*, a covered pony trap, to Porto Santo's superb beach.

P.195 ▸ Essentials

▼ The Madeira balloon

Get high in this tethered balloon rising above the harbour.

P.54 ▸ Central Funchal

▲ Parque Temático, Santana

Seven hectares of multimedia pavilions, rides and children's attractions.

P.169 ▸ Northern and central Madeira

▲ The Lido

A fine escape for children, with rocks to scrabble on and safe bathing pools.

P.74 ▸ Western Funchal and the Hotel Zone

Weird and wonderful

Madeira's last eruption fizzled out 890,000 years ago, but its geological origins are still evident in its bold and occasionally weird landscape, in which former volcanic peaks are punctuated with dramatic cliffs, caves and plateaus. Portuguese settlers have added to these natural wonders with a network of *levadas*, road tunnels and monuments. The most familiar artificial wonder is probably the Santana house, still common on the north coast.

▼ Grutas de São Vicente

Ancient lava flows have left a warren of textured underground caverns buried in the hills outside São Vicente.

P.159 ▶ Porto Moniz and the northwest

▼ Santana houses

The highly practical and picturesque Santana houses still house the odd family, though most are now used for cattle.

P.168 ▶ Northern and central Madeira

▼ Cabo Girão

Peer right down a sheer drop from the top of the world's second-highest sea cliffs.

P.107 ▶ Northwest of Funchal

▲ Paúl da Serra

Driving across these high moors through mist is an eerie experience; when the weather clears, the views are superb.

P.147 ▶ The west

▲ Terreiro da Luta

A towering monument commemorating the end of World War I, set high on a slope above Funchal.

P.98 ▶ Monte and northeast of Funchal

▲ Espada

Ugly as sin, but this delicious deep-water fish is a Madeiran staple.

P.196 ▶ Essentials

Historic Madeira

Madeira was settled in the fifteenth century by the Portuguese; they established lucrative sugar plantations, and soon the island became a major trading post. In the early seventeenth century, the wine trade, backed by powerful British merchants, led to the emergence of a wealthy elite, who also prospered from local embroidery and basket-weaving. But the majority of the islanders lived a harsh existence until the late twentieth century, when tourism and EU funds gave the island a leg-up into the modern age.

▲ Old Blandy's Wine Lodge

The oldest wine lodge on the island, dating back to the early seventeenth century.

P.56 ▸ Central Funchal

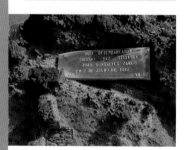

▲ Machico

The island's capital from 1440 to 1496, Machico was the first place on the island to be colonized.

P.118 ▸ Southeastern Madeira

▼ Monte

An important pilgrimage spot, in the mid-
1800s the cool heights of Monte also
became the favoured destination for the
island's first tourists, who stopped en route
to and from Africa and the Americas.

P.93 ▶ Monte and northeast of
Funchal

▼ The Hotel Zone

The island's first luxury hotel, *Reid's* has
welcomed many an illustrious guest,
including Winston Churchill, and blazed a
trail for the plethora of modern hotels that
ensure tourism remains Madeira's main
source of income today.

P.69 ▶ Western Funchal and the
Hotel Zone

▲ Lauraceous forests

The island's ancient laurel woods, protected
by UNESCO, are unique to this corner of
the world.

P.169 ▶ Northern and central
Madeira

▲ Antiga Alfândega

Located on the major shipping routes,
Madeira thrived on international trade,
though much of this former customs house
was destroyed in the earthquake of 1748.

P.51 ▶ Central Funchal

Unspoilt villages

To experience Madeira at its tranquil best means a visit to one of its idyllic villages, where life goes on pretty much as it always has. Hotels are gradually opening in some of these places, too, offering the chance to savour village life after the tour coaches have gone.

▲ Ponta do Sol

With its own little beach, Ponta do Sol is wedged into a valley swathed in banana plantations.

P.140 ▶ The west

▲ São Vicente

Its leafy pedestrianized streets make São Vicente one of the most picturesque spots on the island.

P.158 ▶ Porto Moniz and the northwest

▼ Porto da Cruz

A spectacularly sited north-coast village with its own sea pools.

P.132 ▶ Northeastern Madeira

▼ Câmara de Lobos

This earthy fishing village – Churchill's favourite – has atmosphere by the truckload.

P.104 ▶ Northwest of Funchal

▲ Jardim do Mar

A tranquil village with a burgeoning surf culture, set at the foot of towering cliffs.

P.142 ▶ The west

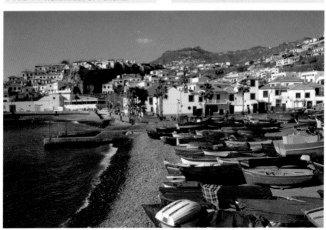

Shopping

The majority of Madeira's goods have to be imported from mainland Portugal, so, not surprisingly, the best-value items are those produced locally, notably wicker, embroidery, tapestry and knitwear. Souvenirs of the edible kind include *bolo de mel* (a spiced caked made from dried fruit and molasses), jars of honey and *pastéis de nata* (Portuguese custard tarts). Madeira wine is the most popular purchase, and Funchal has several *adegas* where you can sample the produce before you buy.

▲ Quinta da Boa Vista

Orchid plants and seedlings can be purchased here and packed and sealed for the journey home.

P.88 ▶ Eastern Funchal and the Old Town

▲ Old Blandy's Wine Lodge

Find out how Madeira is made, then purchase the island's famous tipple.

P.56 ▶ Central Funchal

▼ Mercado, Santa Cruz

Rated the best on the island for fish, this
market is another fine place to purchase
local ingredients.

P.118 ▶ Southeastern Madeira

▲ O Relógio, Camacha

Wicker products galore are sold in this shop
in the mountains above Funchal.

P.116 ▶ Southeastern Madeira

◀ Mercado dos Lavradores

Funchal's bustling
crafts, fruit, fish and
vegetable market shows
off the island's rich
natural produce.

P.83 ▶ Eastern
Funchal and the
Old Town

▶ Casa do Turista

Part museum, part shop,
this place sells a whole
variety of traditional produce, from ceramics to
liqueurs.

P.63 ▶ Central
Funchal

Hotels

Ever since *Reid's* opened towards the end of the nineteenth century, Madeira has had a reputation for top-quality accommodation, and the majority of the island's hotels are rated four stars and over. Many are in the so-called Hotel Zone just west of central Funchal, but there are plenty of options elsewhere, too, including country houses, luxury inns, spa resorts and inexpensive guesthouses.

▲ Quinta Bela São Tiago

A perfect hideaway, with all creature comforts, in the heart of Funchal's Old Town.

P.89 › Eastern Funchal and the Old Town

▲ Cliff Bay

The *Cliff Bay* is typical of the new breed of modern, luxurious hotels, ideal for families.

P.75 › Western Funchal and the Hotel Zone

▼ Reid's Palace Hotel

One of the world's great hotels where tradition is the key word.

P.77 ▸ Western Funchal and the Hotel Zone

▲ Royal Savoy

De luxe apartments for the rich and style-conscious.

P.78 ▸ Western Funchal and the Hotel Zone

◄ Quinta do Arco, Arco de São Jorge

Rural self-catering at its best, near Portugal's largest rose gardens.

P.176 ▸ Northern and central Madeira

► Luamar, Porto Santo

Great family-friendly apartments virtually on the beach.

P.186 ▸ Porto Santo

Cool Madeira

Madeira has a slightly stuffy image, reinforced by its associations with the likes of Winston Churchill and old-fashioned wines. Yet the island is far from being exclusively about crusted ports and crusty people. Its university helps promote a lively young scene, while top architects and designers have added modern flare to the island's traditional styles.

▲ Café do Museu

A cool watering hole for hip Funchalense.

P.67 ▶ Central Funchal

▲ Estalagem Quinta da Casa Branca

An architect's showpiece hotel surrounded by tropical vegetation.

P.76 ▶ Western Funchal and the Hotel Zone

▼ Estalagem da Ponta do Sol

Surreal swimming on a clifftop high above Ponta do Sol.

P.149 ▶ The west

▼ Porto Santo Golf

The best of the new generation of buildings on Porto Santo, combining contemporary design and tradition.

P.184 ▶ Porto Santo

▲ Choupana Hills

Up in the hills and up there with the best of Europe's chic spa resorts.

P.101 ▶ Monte and northeast of Funchal

▲ Crowne Plaza Resort

Philippe Starck furniture and modernism confront you at every turn in this stylish hotel.

P.76 ▶ Western Funchal and the Hotel Zone

Cafés and bars

Virtually every village in Madeira has at least one bar or café, usually open from around 8am to 10pm, sometimes later in the larger resorts. Outside Funchal, cafés often double up as the local shop. The distinction between cafés and bars is blurred; you can usually get a coffee, beer or a glass of wine in both. Even the most basic place will serve simple food such as sandwiches; the larger ones will serve full meals. In Funchal, many cafés and bars play the latest sounds, show live soccer on TV in the corner, or have karaoke or live music.

▲ Bar Gel Burger

A coffee inside or table under the palms at *Bar Gel Burger* is the best place to sample Porto Santo's laid-back lifestyle.

P.188 ▶ Porto Santo

▶ Café do Teatro

Drinks, snacks, ice creams and luvvies: the best place to be seen in Funchal.

P.65 ▶ Central Funchal

◀ Pátio

The photographic museum café has seats in a wonderful courtyard.

P.65 ▶ Central Funchal

▶ O Molhe

A great position, stunning views, music and dance: this place has the lot.

P.80 ▶ Western Funchal and the Hotel Zone

◀ Golden Gate

A slice of colonial Madeira: grab a seat on the balcony for bird's eye views.

P.65 ▶ Central Funchal

Restaurants

Madeira has a good range of places to eat, from tiny backstreet cafés to upmarket restaurants facing the sea. Places geared to tourists – in particular hotel restaurants – tend to serve expensive, high-quality international cuisine. You'll find better-value and more authentic Madeiran cuisine, especially outside Funchal, at smaller restaurants such as *marisqueiras*, specializing in seafood, and *churrascarias*, which serve grills. The average price for a main course with cover and wine is around €16 per person. Anything much less than this is described in the guide as inexpensive, anything over €20, as expensive.

▲ Xoupana, Choupana Hills

A slick restaurant offering fusion and eastern-inspired dining with views to die for.

P.103 ▶ Monte and northeast of Funchal

▼ Arsénio's

Sizzling grills, with a chance to develop a taste for fado.

P.91 ▶ Eastern Funchal and the Old Town

▲ Quinta Furão

Restaurant views don't come better than this, and the food comes a close second.

P.177 ▶ Northern and central Madeira

▼ Solar do Infante

Sleek and good-value beachside dining by Vila Baleira's jetty.

P.190 ▶ Porto Santo

▲ Cervejaria Beerhouse

By night, Funchal's hillside forms a glittering backdrop to the *Cervejaria Beerhouse*'s home-brewed beer and delicious Madeiran cuisine.

P.66 ▶ Central Funchal

Places

Central Funchal

The island's capital, Funchal, is dramatically sited, overlooking the Atlantic from its natural amphitheatre, surrounded by mountains: head any distance inland and you'll be climbing dramatically uphill. The natural magnet for visitors is the extensive seafront, Avenida do Mar. At one end is the marina, the departure point for boat trips around the island, and buzzing with restaurants and cafés. Inland is the historic centre, a series of graceful streets lined with shops, museums and gardens, radiating out from the Sé (cathedral) and the Praça do Município, the main square.

Avenida do Mar

Funchal's main seaside drag is broad, palm-fringed Avenida do Mar, lined with kiosk cafés, most overlooking the town beach. With its ash-like black sand, the beach isn't especially appealing, but it's a pleasant enough place to sit and watch the crashing waves.

Opposite the central stretch of beach is the **Antiga Alfândega**, the old customs house, a relic from Funchal's days of thriving international trade and now the seat of Madeira's regional parliament. The original Renaissance building was largely destroyed in the Great Earthquake of 1748, though some features, such as a Manueline doorway at the northern end, have survived.

Also on the Avenida stands a small stone column, all that remains of **Banger's Tower**.

▲ FUNCHAL

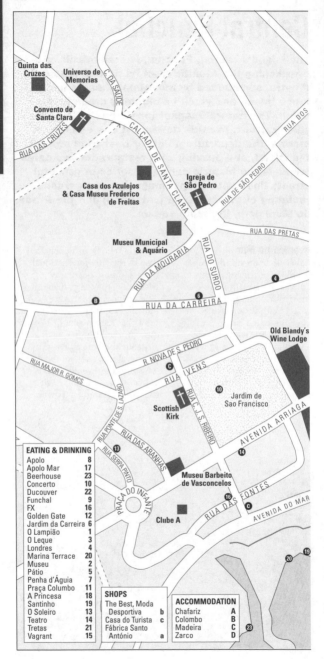

Quinta das Cruzes

Universo de Memorias

C. DA SAUDE

Convento de Santa Clara

CALÇADA DE SANTA CLARA

RUA DAS CRUZES

RUA DOS

Casa dos Azulejos & Casa Museu Frederico de Freitas

Igreja de São Pedro

RUA DE SÃO PEDRO

RUA DAS PRETAS

Museu Municipal & Aquário

RUA DA MOURARIA

RUA DO SURDO

B

6

4

RUA DA CARREIRA

Old Blandy's Wine Lodge

R. NOVA DE S. PEDRO

RUA MAJOR R. GOMCS

RUA IVENS

C

10

Jardim de Sao Francisco

RUA PONTE DE S. LAZARO

RUA C. J.S RIBEIRO

Scottish Kirk

AVENIDA ARRIAGA

RUA DAS ARANHAS

RUA SERPA PINTO

13

14

Museu Barbeito de Vasconcelos

AVENIDA DO MAR

DAS FONTES

16

C

PRAÇA DO INFANTE

Clube A

19

20

23

EATING & DRINKING

Apolo	8
Apolo Mar	17
Beerhouse	23
Concerto	10
Ducouver	22
Funchal	9
FX	16
Golden Gate	12
Jardim da Carreira	6
O Lampião	1
O Leque	3
Londres	4
Marina Terrace	20
Museu	2
Pátio	5
Penha d'Águia	7
Praça Columbo	11
A Princesa	18
Santinho	19
O Soleiro	13
Teatro	14
Tretas	21
Vagrant	15

SHOPS

The Best, Moda Desportiva	b
Casa do Turista	c
Fábrica Santo António	a

ACCOMMODATION

Chafariz	A
Colombo	B
Madeira	C
Zarco	D

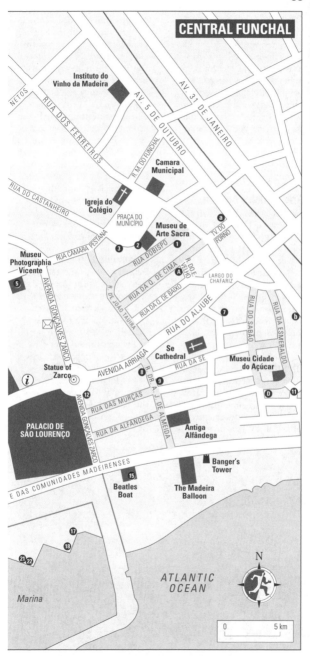

CENTRAL FUNCHAL

Instituto do Vinho da Madeira

AV. 5 DE OUTUBRO

AV. 31 DE JANEIRO

NETOS

RUA DOS FERREIROS

R.M. DO FUNCHAL

Camara Municipal

RUA DO CASTANHEIRO

Igreja do Colégio

PRAÇA DO MUNICÍPIO

Museu de Arte Sacra ❶

TV DO FORNO ⓐ

RUA CAMARA PESTANA

❸ ❷

RUA DO BISPO

Museu Photographia Vicente

❺

R. DE JOÃO TAVIRA

RUA DA Q. DE CIMA

R. DA E. VELHO

ⓐ

RUA DA Q. DE BAIXO

LARGO DO CHAFARIZ

AVENIDA GONÇALVES ZARCO

RUA DO ALJUBE

❼

RUA DO SABÃO

RUA DA ESMERALDO

ⓑ

Se Cathedral

❽ ❾

RUA DA SE

Museu Cidade do Açúcar

AVENIDA ARRIAGA

R. DR. A. J. DE ALMEIDA

ⓓ ⓫

Statue of Zarco ⓘ

❿

⓬

RUA DAS MURÇAS

PALACIO DE SÃO LOURENÇO

AVENIDA GONÇALVES ZARCO

RUA DA ALFÂNDEGA

Antiga Alfândega

E DAS COMUNIDADES MADEIRENSES

⓯

Banger's Tower

Beatles Boat

The Madeira Balloon

⓱

⓲

㉑㉒

ATLANTIC OCEAN

N

Marina

0   5 km

54

Central Funchal **PLACES**

The original structure, some 30m high and nearly 3m in diameter, was one of the city's most distinctive landmarks. It was built in 1798 by a British merchant, John Banger, as a kind of crane for loading ships' cargo and later became a signpost to let market traders know what goods incoming ships were bringing in. In 1939, despite protests, the tower was demolished to make way for the Avenida do Mar.

The Madeira Balloon

Avenida do Mar. Daily every 15min, 9am–9pm. €15, children under 14 €10. A good way to get your bearings in the centre is to take a ride on the Madeira Balloon, a tethered balloon that rises high enough to give you spectacular views over the cruise ships in the harbour. A ride after dark is fun, when the city is lit up below and around you like a magic carpet.

The marina

The attractive marina, with its sleek yachts and terraced restaurants, is one of the liveliest spots in the city, certainly after dark. When there is a big soccer game on, locals crowd the pavements outside any place with a TV; at other times, expect a hard sell from prowling waiters. This is also the place to head for boat trips, with ticket stalls lined up at the marina's eastern end.

Moored nearby is *The Vagrant*, more popularly known as the *Beatles Boat*, a luxury yacht built in the USA for the millionaire Horace Vanderbilt and owned for a time by the Beatles. Sold to a Madeiran businessman, in 1982 it was moored in its present position and turned into the city's kitschest café-restaurant (see p.67).

Palácio de São Lourenço

Entrance on Avenida Gonçalves Zarco. Free visits on Wed at 10am & Fri at 3pm; booking advisable on ☎291 202 530. With its distinctive white facade and single tower, the Palácio de São Lorenço is one of Funchal's most impressive and historic buildings. Today it is the official residence of the Minister of the Republic for Madeira – basically Madeira's MP in the Portuguese government. The original palace was built by the first captains of Madeira,

▲ THE MARINA

though most of the present structure dates back to the period of Spain's brief occupation of Portugal in the sixteenth century. The east wing belongs to the army, but visitors are allowed into the Minister's state rooms in the west wing.

Highlights include the **Ballroom**, full of priceless antiques, including Louis XV mirrors and Louis XVI chairs. The Red Room houses several ornaments from the Ajuda Palace in Lisbon built by Dona Maria II and Dom Ferdinand, nineteenth-century royals who had a penchant for over-the-top, generally tasteless artefacts.

The **Bulwark Room** was one of the last rooms Marcelo Caetano – the successor to the dictator Salazar – used before he was exiled to Brazil following Portugal's peaceful revolution of 1974. The residents of Funchal gave him a hard time, heckling him with cat-calls during his brief stay.

▲ PALÁCIO DE SÃO LOURENÇO

Museu Barbeito de Vasconcelos

Avda Arriaga 48. Mon–Fri 10am–1pm & 3–6pm, Sat 9.30am–1.30pm. €1. The basement of Diogos Wine Shop hides one of Funchal's quirkier museums, the Museu Barbeito de Vasconcelos, the private collection of a local who had a passion both for Madeira and all things to do with Christopher Columbus. The rather rambling collection

Zarco

Avenida Arriaga is graced by the Monumento João Gonçalves Zarco, a statue of the discoverer of Madeira by local artist Francisco Franco. João Gonçalves gained his nickname Zarco ("one-eyed") after he lost an eye fighting the Moors while he was a knight serving Henry the Navigator during Portugal's Golden Age of global expansion in the early fifteenth century. The king decided to entrust Zarco with a mission to explore the coast off Guinea. Zarco set sail in 1418 with another captain, Tristão Vaz Teixeira, but as they headed south their boat was blown off course. They fetched up on Porto Santo, and saw a densely wooded island beyond, which they called Ilha da Madeira – "island of wood". They reported back to Dom Henrique on their findings and two years later returned to Machico and made the previously uninhabited island their home. Zarco became the island's governor, settling in Funchal on the site of the current-day Quinta das Cruzes. Zarco's descendants continued to be governors of the island until the Spanish occupation of 1580. The navigator's remains lie buried in Funchal's Convento de Santa Clara.

consists of paintings, poems, opera scores and books relating mostly to Columbus's first voyage to America but also to his time in Madeira and Porto Santo. Among the displays are a copy of the first work written on Columbus in 1576, as well as a series of portraits of the explorer dating from the seventeenth to the twentieth centuries. Unless you're particularly interested in Columbus, you'll get more out of the collection of old maps, historical prints, postcards of and books about Madeira itself, including *Invalid's Guide to Madeira* of 1840 written by a surgeon, William White; and *An Historical Sketch of the Island of Madeira* dating from 1819.

Jardim de São Francisco

The leafy expanse of the Jardim de São Francisco was once part of the Convento de São

Francisco, and some of the convent ruins are still visible amid the jungle of frangipani, tulip trees and ferns. The gardens also have a delightful series of ponds and fountains. In the north of the park there is a good kiosk café (see p.64), set next to a concrete amphitheatre that occasionally hosts live concerts. The neighbouring Scottish Kirk is an attractive wooden church built in 1861 and still serving the local Presbyterian community.

Old Blandy's Wine Lodge

Avda Arriaga 28. Mon–Fri 9.30am–6.30pm, Sat 10am–1pm; free. Tours Mon–Fri 10.30am, 2.30pm, 3.30pm & 4.30pm, Sat 11am. €4. Set in the Adegas de São Francisco, this is Funchal's oldest wine lodge, where you can sample and buy some of the big names in Madeira wine: Blandy, Miles, Leacock and Cossart Gordon. Parts of the building date from a sixteenth-century Franciscan monastery which stood here before the order was banned from Portugal in the nineteenth century. The present structure is mostly seventeenth century. Incorporated into the grounds is one of Funchal's oldest streets, dating back to the fifteenth century, and along which casks would once have been taken to the harbour.

Though you can wander round a series of atmospheric shops and tasting rooms at will, it is worth joining one of the entertaining and informative hour-

▲ THE SÉ

▲ THE SÉ ROOF

long tours which include visits to rooms otherwise closed to the public. Among them is a series of low-ceilinged chambers where top Madeiras mature in vast wooden barrels, some as high as 3m and holding up to 9000 litres of wine. Guides explain the processes behind making the best Madeiran wines, such as the 1908 Bual, which spent 76 years ageing in a cask and costs over €500 per bottle. The tour ends back in the bar where you get the chance to sample the various wines you have seen maturing.

The Sé

Entrance on Rua da Sé. Free. Funchal's cathedral, the Sé, was built between 1485 and 1514. Its dark basalt-stone exterior and narrow windows are typical of southern European Gothic architecture, though it also has a number of homegrown features, most notably its chequered tiled roof. Around the back of the church are spiralling turrets, typical of Manueline architecture. The most striking feature inside is the geometric patterned wood and ivory ceiling, of unmistakable Moorish inspiration and somewhat at odds with the heavy Baroque decoration imposed on the rest of the interior.

Museu Cidade do Açucar

Praça Colombo 5. Mon–Fri 10am–12.30pm & 2–6pm. €1.50. The Museu Cidade do Açucar is devoted to the history of the island's sugar trade. Most of the collection is fairly dull and consists of sixteenth-century ceramics, religious icons, fifteenth-century sugar moulds and other items connected to the industry that launched Madeira's economy until wine took over.

Of more interest is the building, which occupies the site of what is popularly known as "Columbus's House", though it's believed that Columbus only stayed here briefly in 1498 as a guest of the owner, a sugar merchant, João Esmeraldo, before he set sail for the Americas. The original house was demolished in 1876, then excavated in 1986, revealing several important archeological finds, including the house's original well, given pride of place in the museum.

Instituto do Vinho da Madeira

Entrance on Rua 5 de Outubro. Wine Museum: Mon–Fri 9am–noon & 2–6pm. Free. The towered Instituto do Vinho da Madeira was designed by eccentric British consul Henry Veitch in the nineteenth century and now houses an important institution, which declares the vintage years for all Madeira wine. The institute's **wine museum**, accessed via the central courtyard, contains a mildly interesting collection of grape-picking baskets, barrel scales and corking machines. There are, however, some wonderfully evocative black and white photos of the *borracheiros*, the so-called "drunken" men, whose job it was to carry the hefty goatskins of wine across the island from the farms to the capital; unsurprisingly, they drank a little of their burden to keep them going on the way.

Praça do Município

Praça do Município, the main square, is one of Funchal's prettiest, with a fountain at its centre, red-flowering tulip trees in one corner and in another some fine examples of the extraordinary kapok tree, the pods of which explode into giant cottonwool balls in spring. The east side of the square is dominated by the Câmara Municipal, the town hall, built in 1758 for a local landowner, the Conde de Carvalhal. The guard will happily let you stroll into the central courtyard, beautifully lined with *azulejos*.

Also on the square is the Igreja do Colégio, a rather dour-looking seventeenth-century church. Inside, however, you'll find beautiful *azulejos* dating from the seventeenth and eighteenth centuries.

Museu de Arte Sacra

Rua do Bispo 21. Tues–Sat 10am–12.30pm & 2.30–6pm; temporary exhibits Tues–Sun 10am–1pm & 2–6pm. €3. The Museu de

▲ PRAÇA DO MUNICÍPIO

Arte Sacra, occupying three floors of an eighteenth-century former Bishop's Palace, is one of the finest art galleries in Portugal, let alone Madeira, thanks to its priceless collection of Renaissance

▲ MUSEU DE ARTE SACRA

Flemish paintings. Trading links with Flanders were strong in the fifteenth and sixteenth centuries and there was a ready market for Flemish art among church and government officials and sugar-plantation owners, keen to decorate their chapels. Indeed, wealthy landowners even commissioned their own works of art from Flanders. These artworks remained unprotected and often neglected in private lodgings, chapels and churches around the island until the 1930s, when a restoration programme was undertaken in the Museu de Arte Antiga in Lisbon, and the Museu de Arte Sacra was inaugurated in 1955.

Among the most powerful works are the triptych *Descending from the Cross*, attributed to Gerard David (1518–27), and *The Annunciation*, by Joos Van Cleve (1508–45). Another valuable painting is the *Triptych of Santiago Menor and São Filipe*, by Pieter Coecke Van Aelst (1527–40); in one of the wings sits Simão Gonçalves de Câmara, grandson of Zarco, discoverer of Madeira. Other highlights are the sixteenth-century wooden sculpture of Christ, believed to be from the Flemish or German school;

and a painting of St Jerónimo pensively fingering a skull, attributed to Marinus Van Reymerswaele (1521–40).

The rest of the collection contains Portuguese art from the sixteenth to the eighteenth centuries, while on the first floor you'll find some fine Indo–Portuguese applied arts, including stunning Indian eucharist dishes in mother-of-pearl.

Museu Fotografia Vicentes

Rua da Carreira 43. Mon–Fri 10am–12.30pm & 2–5pm. €2. Entered via a superb balconied courtyard, the Museu Fotografia Vicentes marks the site of Portugal's first-ever photographic studio, set up by Vicente Gomes da Silva in 1865. As a pioneering photographer, da Silva had access to an extraordinary range of people. His clients included Empress Elizabeth of Austria and the Empress of Brazil, and he and his sons managed to photograph nearly every person of note who visited the island at the end of the nineteenth century. Photos of Churchill's visit to Câmara dos Lobos in 1950 also feature, as do shots of the first car on the island (1904)

60

▲ MUSEU FOTOGRAFIA VICENTES

and the first regular seaplane, from Southampton (1949). Some of the most interesting of the family's astonishing collection of 380,000 negatives, however, are those that illustrate everyday life on the island in bygone years: bullock carts being used as public transport, sailing ships visiting the harbour, society figures, as well as ordinary people.

PLACES

Central Funchal

Museu Municipal and Aquário

Tues–Fri 10am–6pm, Sat & Sun noon–6pm. €2.20. The Museu Municipal is mostly given over to a rather old-fashioned natural history collection, which does, however, give a fascinating insight into some of the animal life round the island. The upstairs rooms present a series of skeletons, fossils and stuffed animals native to Madeira, including huge rays, giant monk seals, whales and a crab the size of a small dog. Downstairs is a small, gloomy aquarium, containing a collection of sea creatures native to Madeira's shores, including moray eels and giant snails.

Igreja de São Pedro

Rua de São Pedro. Built between the sixteenth and eighteenth centuries, the Igreja de São Pedro is one of the most beautiful churches in Funchal, with an ornate Baroque altar, painted wooden ceiling and low chandeliers. Most striking are

Carnival

Carnival in Funchal (February or March) is one of Madeira's most important events of the year. Heavily influenced by Rio, with Brazilian music and risqué outfits, it is also gaining a reputation as one of the best carnivals in Europe.

The festivities kick off on the Friday with children from the local primary schools parading in fancy dress. As darkness falls local lads borrow their sisters' or mothers' garb before hitting town for "Transvestite Night".

Saturday evening is when the main parade takes place. At around 9pm, a procession of floats weaves down Avenida do Infant to Avenida Ariaga, before ending up on Praça do Município, the venue for the rest of the evening's music and partying. The floats are entertaining, and the streets around, lined with stalls selling *bolo de caco* and coloured balloons, are highly atmospheric.

Sunday and Monday have more low-key events, with live music in Praça Município during the evening, but things really get going again on Tuesday with the Great Allegorical Parade, open to anyone to participate in and starting at around 4pm, usually processing from the market to the Jardim de São Francisco. Most people wear fancy dress and the whole of Funchal takes on a party atmosphere and coloured streamers cover the streets along the parade route. At around 6pm, there is a farewell-to-carnival show in Praça do Município, with prizes given to the best carnival costumes.

the *azulejos tapetes*, a blue and white geometric carpet of tiles on the walls dating back to the seventeenth century.

Casa dos Azulejos and Casa Museu Frederico de Freitas

Calçada de Santa Clara. Tues–Sat 10am–12.30pm & 2–5.30pm, Sun 10am–12.30pm. €2. The **Casa dos Azulejos** is a wonderful little museum containing tiles from all round the world. On the ground floor are some well-preserved examples from medieval times. Successive floors display exquisitely decorated tiles from Spain, Persia, Turkey, Holland and Syria dating from the twelfth to the nineteenth centuries; Portuguese *azulejos* rescued from demolished buildings on the island; and some particularly fine sixteenth-century mosaics taken from the Convento de Santa Clara.

The neighbouring **Casa Museu Frederico de Freitas**, occupying the attractive eighteenth-century Casa Calçada, contains miscellaneous objects collected by twentieth-century lawyer and veteran traveller, Dr Frederico de Freitas. The house has been renovated in the style of a nineteenth-century *quinta*. Most of the furnishings come from de Freitas's private collection and include oriental carpets, antique furniture from Britain and Portugal and religious paintings, along with collections of Chinese porcelain and Portuguese and English ceramics.

Convento de Santa Clara

Calçada de Santa Clara. Mon–Sat 10am–noon & 3–5pm. €2. The atmospheric Convento de Santa Clara is a working convent, with ancient chapels and beautiful *azulejos*. It was founded in 1496 by Zarco's grandson, João Gonçalves de Camara, whose sister Dona Isabel was the first Abbess. Most of the original convent was destroyed in a pirate attack in 1566, and the nuns fled to Curral das Freiras (see p.110). The present building was constructed in the seventeenth century and still has twenty nuns in residence; if you ring the bell during visiting hours someone will show you round. Up until the nineteenth century, the order was closed, and the young girls

▲ CONVENTO DE SANTA CLARA

sent here by their parents were permitted no contact at all with the outside world. You can still see the thick wooden grille between the church and the nun's private quarters, behind which the girls were confined. During the nineteenth century, conditions were relaxed slightly and the nuns were allowed to make and sell sugar sweets to the congregation, and eventually to tourists.

There are two cloisters – one now contains a children's playground, while the other is particularly peaceful and beautiful, filled with plants and orange trees. Adjacent to the cloisters, the church, spared the pirate attack in 1566, and lined with seventeenth century *azulejos*, contains the tomb of Zarco (see box on p.55).

Quinta das Cruzes

Calçada do Pico 1. Tues–Sat 10am–12.30pm & 2–5.30pm, Sun 10am–1pm. €2, gardens free. The seventeenth-century estate of Quinta das Cruzes was once the private home of a Genoese wine-shipping family, the Lomelinos. The mansion bears testimony to the wealthy lifestyle wine-merchants enjoyed on Madeira at that time and to the importance of Portuguese traders globally. The house overflows with art and silks from India and China, Flemish paintings (including Jean de Mabuse's *Three Magi*), French tapestry, English furniture and nineteenth-century jewellery. There is also a large collection of silver and china pieces, mostly dating from the eighteenth and nineteenth centuries, when the Portuguese shipped porcelain from China to Europe on a large scale. Many of the pieces were made to order and decorated with family coats of arms, or biblical and mythological themes.

Outside, the estate's gardens are also outstanding, a verdant array of flowers and dragon trees forming a superb backdrop to a somewhat esoteric gathering of tombstones, statues and stone window frames that have been rescued from various demolished buildings throughout the island. Some of these are remnants of Zarco's house, which stood on this site before the current *quinta* was built.

Universo de Memórias

Calçada do Pico. Tues–Sat 10am–noon & 2–5pm, Sun 10am–noon. €3. Set in a superb nineteenth-century town house, this museum houses the eclectic belongings of obsessive collector João Carlos Abreu, the Madeiran minister for tourism and former journalist and travel agent. His extensive travels are evident, with many pieces from the Middle East and Orient. Not all of the stuff is valuable and some is downright tacky, but the range is astonishing: modern surrealist art, fifteenth-century porcelain, masks, jewellery, vases,

▲ PASTEL DE NATA AND COFFEE

paintings, even Abreu's mum's hats and his own substantial array of ties. Upstairs there is an entire floor dedicated to his collection of horses, from funfair models to Victorian rocking horses and Murano crystal stallions. Much of the appeal of the place is the house itself, whose original features include stained-glass windows and wooden floors. There is also a tea room in the small gardens at the back.

Fortaleza do Pico

Rua do Castelo. Mon–Fri 9am–6pm. Free. Bus #15A from Praça da Autonomia. If you're feeling energetic, it's well worth climbing the very steep hill to Fortaleza do Pico for the stunning views back over the city. The fort was built in 1611 when Madeira was under Spanish rule and is now used by the navy; the only part open to the public is a room showing prints of the building over the years, though you are free to wander round the front ramparts and enjoy the views.

Hotels

Residencial Chafariz

Rua do Estanco Velho 3–5 ☎291 232 260, ⊕291 232 250. Central and quiet, on a narrow pedestrianized street opposite the Sé. Good-sized rooms come complete with cable TV and en-suite bathrooms. The fourth-floor breakfast room has great views over the town. €44.

Residencial Colombo

Rua do Carreira 182 ☎291 225 231/2, ⊕291 222 170. A modern, ungainly-looking guesthouse at the west end of Rua do Carreira, but rooms are good value, with phones, TV and private bathroom, and there's also a sunny roof terrace. The upper-floor rooms have views over the sea. €44.

Hotel Madeira

Rua Ivens 21 ☎291 230 071, ⊛www .hotelmadeira.com. A white, modern building with red-faced, angled balconies in an attractive position near the Jardim de São Francisco. The rooms are small but well equipped and include satellite TV, while elsewhere there's a bar, a billiard lounge and a rooftop pool. Pretty good value for such a central location. €66.

Residencial Zarco

Rua da Alfândega 113 ☎ & ⊕291 223 716, ⊛ifo@residencialzarco .com. A large, friendly *residencial* with slightly shabby rooms, each with its own shower and TV. Rooms (€25) at the front can be noisy, but the position just by the seafront can't be faulted. It also lets out apartments with kitchenettes at a nearby annexe for €30.

Shops

The Best, Moda Desportiva

Rua 5 Outubro 16–17. Mon–Fri 9am–7.30pm, Sat 9am–1pm. This small sports shop is the perfect place to stock up on walking gear before hitting the *levadas*, with a range of good-quality walking boots and sticks.

Casa do Turista

Rua do Conselheiro José Silvestre Ribeiro 2. Mon–Fri 9.30am–1pm & 2.30–6.30pm, Sat 9.30am–1pm. Part museum, part handicrafts shop, set inside a period building. The nineteenth-century decor is impressive, though the "traditional" produce on offer – ceramics, embroidery, bags, wicker, dolls, silver, quilts, tiles, maps, guides, Madeira wine and liqueurs – is of very mixed quality. There's a small terrace at the back with a mock post office-cum-bar front and a traditional bedroom, perhaps the best part.

Fábrica Santo António
Travessa do Forno 27–29. Mon–Fri 9am–1pm & 2–7pm, Sat 9am–1pm. A wonderful bakery piled high with homemade cakes, biscuits, preserves and croissants.

Cafés

Apolo Mar
Marina de Funchal (no phone). Daily 7am–1am. At the eastern end of the marina, this local café serves grilled fish and meat dishes. There's a TV above the bar and lots of outdoor tables facing the bobbing boats in the marina.

Café Concerto
Jardim de São Francisco ☎291 220 986. Daily 8am–11pm. Offering milkshakes, sandwiches, pastries and fresh fruit juices, including

▲ TAXI DRIVERS ON AVENIDA ARRIAGA

kiwi, mango and papaya, this small kiosk also serves full lunches, *poncho* and wine. The setting is perfect: in the leafy municipal gardens next to the park auditorium and fountains.

Café Funchal

Rua Dr José António Almeida ☏291 222 290. Daily 8am–midnight. One of a cluster of high-profile cafés on this pedestrianized street. Open-fronted, with a counter full of cakes, and shaded outdoor seating under a blue canopy; a great spot to watch the world go by.

Golden Gate

Avenida Arriaga 27–29 ☏291 234 383. Mon–Wed & Sun 8am–midnight, Thurs–Sat 8am–2am. This has been a fashionable meeting place since the nineteenth century, when it was a hotel bar. You can get everything from morning coffee and croissant to ice creams, alcohol and full meals. It was substantially remodelled in 1998, but its decor nevertheless retains a period feel, with lots of mirrors, ceiling fans and wicker chairs. There's also a first-floor balcony and a few outside tables.

O Leque

Praça do Município 7 ☏291 227 229. Mon–Fri 8am–midnight, Sat 9am–1pm. This café's outdoor tables on the lovely town square, with its mosaic pavements and central fountain, are hard to resist. Reasonably priced drinks, snacks and lunches are available.

Pastelaria Penha d'Águia

Rua de João Gago 6–8 ☏291 228 119. Mon–Fri 8am–7pm, Sat 8am–3.30pm. Just round the back of the Sé, this is one of the best places in central Funchal for pastries, with a long stand-up counter groaning with *pastéis*

de nata, cakes, big croissants, *queijada* cheese biscuits, mini pizzas, sandwiches and *sonhos* ("dreams"): small round cakes dipped in dark honey.

Pátio

Rua da Carreira 43 ☏291 227 376. Mon–Sat 8.30am–10pm. A superb spot in the courtyard of the photogenic photographic museum (see p.59), where you can enjoy drinks and ice creams surrounded by plants beneath a wrought-iron balcony. The adjoining restaurant does good-value Madeiran food and snacks.

Café da Praça Columbo

Praça Columbo ☏292 229 582. Daily 8am–8pm. A modern stand-up café-bar kiosk, with outdoor tables spilling out onto the attractive square opposite the Museu Cidade do Açucar. Good fresh juices and coffee are served, as well as Guinness and Coral beer on tap.

Café do Teatro

Avenida Arriaga ☏291 226 371, ⊛www.cafedoteatro.com. Sun–Thurs 8am–2am, Fri–Sat 8am–4am. A fashionable café-bar in a corner of the town theatre, with shaded outdoor tables. Meals are served until 10pm. It's a good place to people-watch, and is one of the few gay-friendly bars in town.

The Vagrant

Avenida do Mar ☏291 223 572. Daily 11am–11pm. Also known as the Beatles Boat (see p.54), although it's hard to know what John, Paul and Co would make of the yacht's current reincarnation as an unashamedly touristy restaurant-café-bar. The tables out on deck overlooking the beach are the best, though you can also sit in one of numerous mini-boats set in shallow water and "enjoy eating with the sensation of navigating" as the publicity promises. The food itself – Portuguese dishes as well as pizza, pasta, pastries and ice cream – is very average, though it's a fine place for a drink, and kids love it. The night-time lights add to the impression that this place is so kitsch it is almost cool.

Restaurants

Apolo

Rua Dr J. António Almeida 21 ☎291 220 099. Daily 8am–11pm. A high-profile restaurant and café on a pedestrianized street linking the Sé with the seafront. The extensive menu is surprisingly reasonable with a long list of starters and good fish and meat main courses. The house salads make an excellent light lunch. It's a popular stopping-off point for locals on their way home from work, though most sit in the rather dull Art Deco interior

leaving the attractive outdoor tables for tourists to sit and watch the world go by.

Cervejaria Beerhouse

Porto de Funchal ☎291 229 011. Daily 10am–midnight. Just above the marina and sporting a distinctive, tent-like roof, this is one of the best restaurants in town thanks to its fine food and superb views of Funchal, with seating inside or out. The long menu offers decent soups, salads and specials such as seafood with *açorda* (bread sauce), lobster and superb tuna, best washed down with the home-brewed unfiltered beer. Full meals cost around €15–20.

Ducouver

Marina de Funchal ☎291 237 050. Daily 10am–1am. The restaurant's terrace affords great views over the marina, though the aggressive marketeering to lure you in can be offputting. The food and service is good, however, with decent pasta,

▲ CENTRAL FLOWER STALL

pizza and superb fresh fish such as *bodião* (parrot fish). Other specialities include *bife na pedra* (steak cooked on a hot stone) and *peixe assado no sal* (fish baked in salt). Around €15–20 for a full meal.

Jardim da Carreira

Rua da Carreira 118 ☎291 222 498. Daily 10am–11pm. Popular with tourists thanks to a superb, tranquil courtyard full of flowers and trees, the *Jardim da Carreira* serves Madeiran staples, such as tomato and onion soup with egg, and *espadarte* (scabbard fish) with banana, as well as good-value set lunches. Main courses are €5–9.

O Lampião

Rua do Bispo 30a ☎291 225 015. Mon–Sat 7.30am–10.30pm. Join the row of workers at the bar for a bargain lunchtime menu. There's also a TV at the back and a couple of outdoor tables in front on the pedestrianized street. Full meals for around €10.

Londres

Rua da Carreira 64a ☎291 235 329. Mon–Sat 11.30am–4pm & 6pm– midnight. A traditional restaurant with uninspiring decor but serving a very good menu, including daily specials, *bacalhau* and other fish dishes (usually sea bream, salmon and trout), along with steaks. Full meals come to €12–15.

Marina Terrace

Marina de Funchal ☎291 230 547. Daily 10am–11pm. With lots of tables on a semi-covered terrace at the west end of the marina, this is probably the best value of the larger restaurants in the area, offering simple and effective dishes such as chicken and beef kebabs, tuna cooked in wine

and garlic and enormous *arroz de mariscos*, plus inexpensive house wine. Full meals cost around €15.

A Princesa

Marina de Funchal ☎291 237 719. Daily 10am–midnight. *A Princesa* avoids the hard sell of the other restaurants along this stretch, perhaps because it can rely on the knowledge that its deliciously chargrilled fresh fish will pull punters back. Don't be put off by something called BSE on the wine list – it's actually rather good. Bargain set lunches start at under €10.

O Soleiro

Rua Serpa Pinto 28 ☎291 229 634. Daily noon–3pm & 6–11pm. *O Soleiro* does very good-value tuna steaks with fried maize and other dishes, along with fine house wines. If you don't fancy a full meal, perch at the bar with the locals, who crowd in when live football is on TV. Full meals around €10–12.

Bars

Café do Museu

Praça Municipio ☎291 281 121. Mon–Sat 10am–2am. Set under the arcades of the Museu de Arte Sacra and attracting a young, arty crowd, this is one of Funchal's hippest hang-outs. Gentle jazzy and contemporary sounds inside, tables facing the square outside and an inventive drinks menu including vodka sherbet. Meals served until 8pm.

FX

Largo das Fontes ☎291 250 806. Daily 6pm–2am. With its entrance and an outdoor terrace just below Avenida do Mar near Palácio de São Lourenço, this is one of

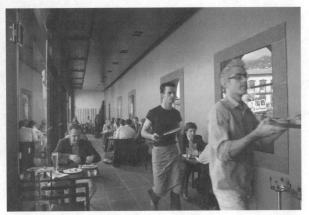

▲ CAFÉ DO MUSEO

Funchal's trendier places, with a sleek, wood floor and a long bar. Attracts a young clientele, expecially when there's a live band (usually at weekends), but doesn't get going till late.

Santinho

Marina do Funchal ℡291 228 945. Dalily 10am–2am. A lively marina-side music bar, with vibrant sounds, sports TV, live music most weekends and a young crowd downing *poncho*, sangria and caipirinhas (Brazilian cocktails). It also does inexpensive snacks, including a filling *prego no bolo do caco* (beef in garlic bread).

Tretas

Marina do Funchal ℡291 237 050 Sun–Thurs 3pm–2am, Fri & Sat 3pm–4am. *Tretas* bills itself as a disco-pub and is certainly the liveliest spot in the marina, with pulsing music and a wide TV screen in one corner often showing live soccer. There are karaoke sessions some nights.

Clubs

Clube A

Marina Shopping, Avenida Arriaga ℡291 281 282. Fri–Sat 10pm–4am. One of the friendlier and more attractive clubs in Funchal, tastefully decorated with laminate flooring and chrome light fittings. Music is an eclectic mix of old and new. Attracts a mainly, but not exclusively, young crowd, and bar prices are reasonable.

Western Funchal and the Hotel Zone

Western Funchal consists largely of the Zona Hoteleira, or Hotel Zone, the area where most visitors to Funchal stay. This is an unashamedly upmarket holiday suburb sprawling along the busy coastal Estrada Monumental, a medley of restaurants, shops and state-of-the-art hotel complexes vying for ocean views. The main attraction is the leafy Jardim de Santa Catarina, the city's largest park. Attractions west of here include a traditional wine producer, the Barbeito wine lodge; the attractive gardens of Quinta Magnolia; and the venerable *Reid's*, one of the world's best-known hotels. Further west sit two enormous lidos and Funchal's main beach, at Praia Formosa.

Jardim de Santa Catarina

Set on a high bluff overlooking the harbour is the city's main park, the Jardim de Santa Catarina, a wonderful swathe of breezy parkland, laid out between 1945 and 1966. There are a couple of sights worth checking out near the main entrance: a small statue of Christopher Columbus and the Capela de Santa Catarina, an attractive (but usually locked) seventeenth-century chapel which sits on the site of an old wooden church commissioned in 1425 by the wife of Zarco (see box on p.55). An expanse of coarse grass above this makes a good picnic spot, with superb views back over the city.

A network of paths leads uphill past plants and succulents and beautiful trees, including red-flowering tulip trees. On the seaside path, enormous cacti, Euforbia Gigante, reach some 15m high. At the top end of the park, a fenced-off area next to two rusting old traction engines marks a children's playground, complete with slides, swings and climbing frames, a must for anyone with kids. Just below the playground there is a small lake and a park café, *Esplanada do Lago*, where you can enjoy cold drinks or ice cream surrounded by palms, bamboos and shady trees.

▲ JARDIM DE SANTA CATARINA

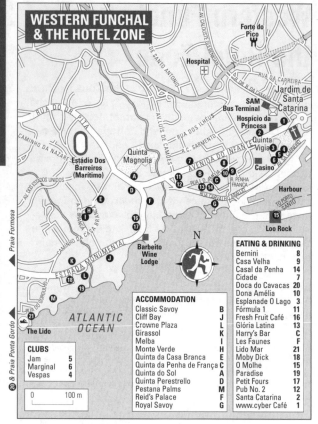

WESTERN FUNCHAL & THE HOTEL ZONE

ACCOMMODATION

Classic Savoy	B
Cliff Bay	J
Crowne Plaza	L
Girassol	K
Melba	I
Monte Verde	H
Quinta da Casa Branca	E
Quinta da Penha de França	C
Quinta do Sol	A
Quinta Perestrello	D
Pestana Palms	M
Reid's Palace	F
Royal Savoy	G

EATING & DRINKING

Bernini	8
Casa Velha	9
Casal da Penha	14
Cidade	7
Doca do Cavacas	20
Dona Amélia	10
Esplanade O Lago	3
Fórmula 1	11
Fresh Fruit Café	16
Glória Latina	13
Harry's Bar	C
Les Faunes	F
Lido Mar	21
Moby Dick	18
O Molhe	15
Paradise	19
Petit Fours	17
Pub No. 2	12
Santa Catarina	2
www.cyber Café	1

CLUBS

Jam	5
Marginal	6
Vespas	4

0   100 m

Quinta Vigia

Avenida do Infante. Mon–Sat
9am–5pm. Free. The pink
eighteenth-century Quinta
Vigia, an attractive but
surprisingly modest building,
is the official residence of
Madeira's president. Formerly
the Quinta Angústias, home of
the Empress of Brazil during
the 1850s, it stepped in to
fill the shoes of the original
Quinta Vigia, controversially
demolished to make way for the
neighbouring *Carlton Park Hotel*
in the 1960s. Visitors are only
allowed to visit the beautiful

eighteenth-century chapel, lined
with superb *azulejos* depicting
the life of Saint Francis, and the
attractive gardens, which contain
peacocks, a parrot enclosure and
more sweeping views over the
harbour.

Hospício da Princesa

Avenida do Infante. Gardens daily
9am–6pm. Free. The attractive
Hospício da Princesa was
founded in 1859 by the Empress
of Brazil in memory of her
daughter, Princess Maria Amélia,
who died of TB in 1853 at the
age of 22. The empress couldn't

bear to have much to do with the hospice and entrusted its running to her sister Josephine, Queen of Sweden. Its luxuriant gardens, full of spiny dragon trees and towering palms, are open to the public.

The casino

Avenida do Infante
☎291 209 185.
Over-18s only.
Mon–Thurs & Sun 3pm–3am, Fri & Sat 4pm–4am.

▲ AZULEJOS, QUINTA VIGIA

Free. Funchal's casino, a little slice of Las Vegas, is part of a complex designed by Brazilian Oscar Niemeyer, the architect of Brasilia, and, like the Brazilian capital, the park is not everyone's cup of tea. The circular casino building resembles a concrete wart and is only marginally less offensive than the park's vast hotel on stilts, the *Carlton Park Hotel*. From 8pm daily, there are games of roulette and black jack, along with cabaret and musical performances.

The harbour and Loo Rock

Offering some of the best views of the city, the **harbour** is a bustling area of colourful fishing boats, container ships loaded with vast crates of bananas, and giant cruise ships which dock early morning most days. It's also the departure point for the daily ferry to Porto Santo

▼ HOSPÍCIO DA PRINCESA GARDENS

▲ FUNCHAL HARBOUR VIEW

(see p.178). Surveying all is the fortress on top of **Loo Rock**, which juts out into the harbour. The rock was where Madeira's settlers spent their first night, feeling more secure here than on the mainland. In 1656, a small fortress was built on the rock, and a chapel to Nossa Senhora da Conceição, currently closed for restoration, was added in 1682. Between 1757 and 1762, the rock was joined to the mainland, the harbour wall was gradually extended and, in 1866, a lighthouse was added. In 1992, the rock passed from the military to the local council, and the fort now houses a café, club and restaurant, *O Molhe* (see p.80 for review), reached by a lift. It's worth having at least a drink in the café to enjoy the views of the city and sea.

Quinta Magnolia

Rua Dr Pita. Daily: May–Sept 8am–9pm; Oct–April 8am–7pm. City bus #5, #6, #8 or #45 from opposite the Marina. Free; pay at main gate for sports facilities. Set in an attractive park and formerly the site of the British Country Club, the leisure complex Quinta Magnolia is an oasis of tranquillity in a busy part of the city. It's a great resource if you're staying somewhere without a pool or gardens. Facilities include a children's playground, tennis courts (€1.75 per person a session) and a large freshwater swimming pool (€1.40), not to mention an attractive café-bar.

Reid's Palace Hotel

Estrada Monumental 139. Bus #1, 2, 6, 24 or 35 from Avenida do Mar. *Reid's* is something of a living legend, one of the world's truly great hotels. Though a night here – or, come to that, a meal at one of its many restaurants – is beyond many people's means, you can get a glimpse of the hotel's lavish interior and enjoy the terrace views by taking afternoon tea (3–5.30pm daily; €23); you'll need to book a day in advance (☎291 717 171).

The hotel was founded by William Reid, the son of a Scottish crofter, born in Kilmarnock in 1822 and one

▲ QUINTA MAGNOLIA

of twelve children. William, a sickly child, was advised to go to warmer climes to improve his health. In 1836, he earned his passage on a ship to Madeira via Lisbon. Once in Funchal, he got a job as a baker and later in the wine trade. A natural entrepreneur, he soon set up an agency catering to wealthy tourists who wanted to stay in local *quintas*, in those days the only places to stay in comfort. Spotting a market, Reid saved enough to buy his own place, *Quinta das Fontes*, and converted it into a hotel. The venture had a powerful backer: the Duke of Edinburgh, and the hotel was appropriately renamed the *Royal Edinburgh Hotel*. Reid soon acquired further hotels and guesthouses, but his ambition was to own a purpose-built establishment, and eventually he managed to buy Salto do Cavalo, a five-acre British-owned estate on a clifftop, 50m above sea level. Sadly, Reid died three years before his dream was realized and the hotel was completed in 1891, designed by George Somers, architect of the *Shepherd's Hotel* in Cairo.

By the early 1900s, *Reid's* had established itself as the centre of Madeira's social life. In 1936, it was taken over by the Blandy family, who added new wings and seawater swimming pools. It's now owned by Orient Express Hotels, who have undertaken further renovation of the building and its gardens.

In the early twentieth century, guests arrived at the hotel's own landing stage by boat or seaplanes. Nowadays, celebrities slip in quietly by car. The list of past guests reads like a who's who of the last century and includes Captain Scott of the Antarctic (1901); Edward VIII; Lloyd George (1925); Churchill (see box on p.107); George Bernard Shaw (1924), who met resident tango instructor Max Rinder and called him "the only man that ever taught me anything"; pioneer flyer Amy Johnson (1933); General Batista of Cuba, fleeing from Castro's revolution in 1958 (and who took over an entire floor of the hotel); Gregory Peck and John Huston, who stayed here while filming Moby Dick's whale-hunting scenes; Portugal's dictator Salazar; James Bond AKA Roger Moore; novelist Frederick Forsyth; and countless heads of state and European royals.

Barbeito Wine Lodge

Estrada Monumental ☎291 761 829. Mon–Fri 9am–12.30pm & 2–5.30pm. Bus #1, 2, 6, 24 or 35 from Avenida do Mar. Tucked away amid some of Funchal's flashest hotels lies this

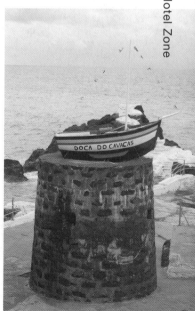

▲ THE SEAFRONT PROMENADE

PLACES

Western Funchal and the Hotel Zone

Madeira wine

In around 1687, a barrel of wine was left forgotten in a corner of a ship for two long sea journeys. When a sailor was allowed to drink the "spoiled" wine, it was discovered that the slow warming of the barrel as the ship passed to and from the tropics had helped mature the wine. These days, this warming effect is re-created in large vats called *estufas*, where wines are kept at temperatures of 40–50°C for three to six months, giving the wines a slightly smoky taste. The wine is then stored for eighteen months before it is transferred into American oak barrels. These barrels are not tightly sealed as air actually improves the Madeira.

Madeira remains fairly unique in its ability to improve with age. Some islanders are said to buy a good Madeiran wine and have a glass of it once a year to celebrate special occasions such as wedding anniversaries, with no noticeable

little low-rise building, home to a very traditional wine producer. Stick your head in the door and you'll be overwhelmed by the warm and heady smell of Madeira wine, and be confronted by giant wine barrels and rattling bottling machines. There's a small tasting room and shop to one side, where you can sample and buy the produce.

The lido

Rua Gorgulho. Daily 8.30am–7pm. €2.70. City bus #6 from Avenida do Mar. Though rather chilly, the Olympic-sized seawater pool in Funchal's municipal lido is a great place to head for a proper swim. When the sea is rough, the waves literally break into the pool; in calm weather you can also climb down ladders to the rocks below and swim in the Atlantic. At the far end of the

lido there is a smaller children's pool, complete with water slides and stepping stones. Built into the cliff face above are cafés, restaurants and shops. It gets pretty packed at weekends, but otherwise makes a fine spot to laze away an afternoon.

Praia Ponta Gordo

Daily: May–Sept 8.30am–8pm; Oct–April 8.30am–7pm. €2.70. Bus #1, 2 or 24 from Avenida do Mar. Praia Ponta Gordo, some fifteen minutes' walk west of the main Lido, is a new lido complex on a broad, flat stretch of coast, comprising sea pools, slides and sunbathing areas; there's also sea access, a café and restaurant.

Praia Formosa

City bus #35 from Avenida do Mar. Beyond Praia Ponta Gordo, the

▼ THE PROMENADE NEAR PRAIA FORMOSA

▲ THE HOTEL ZONE AND WESTERN FUNCHAL

seafront promenade continues west for another 1km or so to Praia Formosa, which is reached via a tunnel blasted through the rock – halfway along it, a rock window looks into a sea cave. Funchal's nearest stretch of proper beach, Praia Formosa is a long expanse of stony shore dotted with palm-frond sunshades. In 1566, the beach was the landing stage for Bertrand de Montluc, a French pirate, whose band of men went on to ransack Funchal. These days the beach's main blight is a Shell petroleum plant; it certainly doesn't win any beauty prizes, but nevertheless it has a refreshingly local feel to it. The best part of the beach is at the western end, where there is a stretch of fine black sand, a summer go-cart track, five-a-side soccer pitch, children's playground and changing facilities. The beach's promenade is popular with locals at weekends, out to take the sea air or on their way to the cafés and restaurants. In summer, there are also watersports, including jet skiing and canoeing.

Hotels

The Cliff Bay

Estrada Monumental 147 ☎291 707 700, ⊛www.cliffbay.com. This stylish, modern hotel is built into a series of terraces spilling down the cliffs. Rooms are plush, with large balconies, and the fluffy dressing gowns are to die for. It's a great place for families; facilities include indoor and outdoor pools, gym, kindergarten, four restaurants and two bars. Tennis, windsurfing, massages and fishing trips can be arranged. Disabled access. €245, or €290 for sea views.

Hotel Classic Savoy

Avenida do Infante ☎291 213 000, ⊛www.savoyresort.com. One of Funchal's older hotels. The communal areas have a nice period feel, but some of the rooms are looking their age, and none comes cheap here, not even the unexceptional ones with "mountain view" – actually overlooking the hotel car park. But the tariffs do cover a vast range of facilities, including inside and outside pools, bars, three restaurants and a garden with golf-driving nets, a giant chess set and a playground. There are also a gym and beauty treatment room. Disabled access. €295, or €345 for a sea view.

Crowne Plaza Resort

Estrada Monumental 175–177 ☎291 717 700, ⊛www.madeira.crowneplaza. com. Though the concrete and glass exterior would turn Prince Charles apoplexic, the rooms and facilities here are on a par with any luxury hotel on the island. There are superb views from the contemporary-designed rooms, all of which have balconies facing the enormous sea terrace, complete with pools and a bar – it's the largest on the island and is reached via glass lifts. Elsewhere you'll find squash, tennis courts, a diving centre and thelassotherapy centre, not to mention restaurants and a cool cocktail bar full of colourful Philippe Starck furniture. Disabled access. €225.

Hotel Girassol

Estrada Monumental 256 ☎291 701 570, ⊛www.maisturismo.pt/girasol. Popular with package-tour operators, this unpromising L-shaped concrete block sits on the wrong side of the Estrada Monumental, with its sea views partially obscured by the Crowne Plaza opposite. Nevertheless, the good-sized rooms and suites can't be faulted, and there are two pools, a bar, restaurant, cable TV, babysitting, a games room, sauna and gym. €75.

Residencial Melba

Azinhaga Casa Branca 8 ☎291 774 072, ℗291 775 515. Probably the best-value place in the Hotel

Zone, sharing the facilities of the Estalagem Monte Verde (see below). Rooms are simple but clean, though a new road out front adds to the noise level. All it lacks is a sea view. €30.

Estalagem Monte Verde

Azinhaga Casa Branca 8 ☎291 774 072, ℗291 775 515. Attached to the Residencial Melba (see aove), this is a good-value, low-rise inn, five minutes' walk uphill from the Hotel Zone. The spacious rooms all have cable TV and balconies, some facing the sea, and there's a small pool at the side. €37.

Pestana Palms

Rua do Gorgulho 15 ☎291 709 200, ⊛www.pestana.com. Set in the lovely grounds of an old quinta, a stone's throw from the main lido. The quinta is now a library, with most of the hotel rooms in a stylish modern block on a clifftop. The plush rooms have kitchenettes and balconies with fantastic sea views, and there's also a restaurant, healthclub, an outdoor pool by the sea and private access to the sea. €168.

Estalagem Quinta da Casa Branca

Rua da Casa Branca 5–7 ☎291 700 770, ⊛www.quintacasabranca .pt. Designed by local architect João Favila, this place has a chic boutiquey feel. It's situated in a tranquil part of town behind a historic family quinta (still privately occupied), and it has substantial grounds full of tropical foliage. Each well-equipped ground-floor room opens onto its own lawnside terrace, while rooms in the new annexe have neat sliding shutters giving onto large balconies. There's also a health centre, pools and a separate restaurant serving gourmet Portuguese food. €165.

Quinta da Penha de França

Rua Imperatriz Dona Amélia ☏291 204 650, ⓦwww.hotelquintapenhafranca.com. This lovely old quinta is squeezed in among larger hotels just above the harbour. There's a mixed bag of good-value rooms, from the small, but cosy, ones with shower in the original building (from €56) to smarter, larger ones in the modern extension, sporting balconies overlooking the small garden and pool (€105). Another set of rooms is to be had at a seaside annexe by the harbour, complete with terrace-balconies (€118).

Quinta Perestrello

Rua do Dr Pita 3 ☏291 706 700, ⓦwww.charminghotelsmadeira.com. Lovely 150-year-old *quinta* set in small grounds with its own pool, restaurant and terrace café. Rooms are airy and wood-floored, with those in the modern extension having their own terraces. The only disadvantage is its position wedged in by a busy road junction. €125, or €150 with a terrace.

Quinta do Sol

Rua do Dr Pita 6 ☏291 707 010, ⓦwww.enotel.com. There's no longer a *quinta* here, just six floors of concrete faced with zigzagged green shutters. The four-star facilities mean large rooms, most with balconies, plus a restaurant, cocktail bar, live entertainment, barbecue nights and a small garden with pool. The upper floors are best for sea views and are further from the adjacent busy road junction. The back rooms don't have balconies, but face the tranquil gardens

of Quinta Magnolia (see p.72). €115, or €125 for sea views.

Reid's Palace Hotel

Estrada Monumental 139 ☏291 717 171, ⓦwww.reidspalace.com. Madeira's first and most famous hotel (see p.72) and rated one of the best hotels in the world. Much of its appeal lies in its rambling size, which manages to absorb any number of visitors without ever seeming full, and its air of tradition that steers a line between charm and fustiness. Its array of facilities includes three restaurants, pools and sea access, a poolside café (see p.78), sweeping views over Funchal, tranquil gardens and an entertainments programme, including special "Fun at *Reid's*" days for children. Rooms are sumptuous and spacious, though nothing beats the Churchill Suite, bigger than some people's houses and complete with pop-up TV at the end of the bed. Some guests return every year, and it's easy to see why. €315.

▲ TEA AT REID'S

Royal Savoy

Rua Carvalho Araújo ☎291 213 500, ⊛www.savoyresort.com. Consisting of 162 enormous suites and large studios, each with kitchenettes and balconies facing the sea, this is one of Funchal's swishest and priciest hotels. Modern rooms are ranged around a lower seafront area replete with palm trees and a series of pools, while lifts whisk you up to facilities that include a spa, tennis courts and restaurants. €450.

Shops

Madeira Shopping

Santa Quitéria, St. António ⊛www .madeirashopping.pt. Shops Sun–Thurs 10am–11pm, Fri & Sat 10am–midnight. City bus #8, 8A, 16 or 50 from Estrada Monumental. Signed off the road to Pico do Barcelos, this is Madeira's largest shopping centre, with 112 national and international shops including Body Shop, Timberland, Mango, Zara, Massimo Dutti and the toy shop Imaginarium. There are also seven cinema screens, and various cafés and restaurants.

Cafés

Bar Santa Catarina

Avenida do Infante 22. Daily 8am–midnight. Unpromisingly positioned, on a busy road at the foot of a modern shopping centre opposite Quinta Vigia, but this café does a mean range of pastries and superb *batidas* (fruit shakes), including pineapple, mango and custard apple.

Esplanade O Lago

Parque de Santa Catarina. Daily: May–Oct 10am–9pm; Nov–April 10am–8pm. A tranquil spot by the park lake and next to the children's play area, where you can enjoy coffees, ice creams or pastries surrounded by palms, bamboos and flowering trees.

Fresh Fruit Café

Estrada Monumental 128. Daily 10am–10pm. The name says it all – it's a very healthy place to stop for fresh fruit, tropical fruit salads and wonderful *batidas*.

Petit Fours

Estrada Monumental 188, Loja 4. Daily 8am–8pm. A modern café offering great croissants, fresh bread and pastries, with a few tables set out on a patio inside the neighbouring shopping centre.

Reid's Palace Hotel Tea Lounge and Terrace

Reid's Palace Hotel, Estrada Monumental 139 ☎291 717 171. Teas daily 3–5.30pm. Not cheap at €23, but a seriously large, traditional English tea, including sandwiches and cake, served on the sea-facing terrace at this world-famous hotel. The best way to mix it with the elite. Reservations 24 hours in advance are essential.

Restaurants

Bernini

Rua Imperatriz D. Amélia 68 ☎291 230 323. Daily noon–2.30pm & 6.30–10.30pm. Just below the casino complex, this is an unpretentious glass-fronted Italian restaurant with a long list of homemade pasta dishes, pizza, salads and Portuguese staples, not to mention a fine passionfruit liqueur. A friendly place and popular with families. Mains from €9.

Casa Velha

Rua Imperatriz D. Amélia 69 ☎291
205 600. Daily 12.30–3pm & 7–11pm.
Set in a nineteenth-century
villa, the *Casa Velha* has a semi-
tropical, colonial feel with
ceiling fans, old prints on the
walls and a luxuriant garden.
It's usually bustling and not too
formal, serving fish, meat and
superb desserts, including crepes
and banana flambés. It's certainly
the most atmospheric of the
restaurants in a little triangle of
traditional buildings behind the
casino complex. Main courses
around €12–15.

Casal da Penha

Rua Penha de França ☎291 227
674. Daily 11am–midnight. The
main draw of this place is
an appealing outside terrace
overlooking a quiet side street.
    The mid-priced food,
including *Lulas a Diabo* (spicy
squid), *Frango piri piri* (chilli
chicken) and crepes, is not bad
either, and there is a long list of
starters and desserts.

Doca do Cavacas

Estrada Monumental ☎291 762 052.
Daily noon–10.30pm. This lovely,
traditional, white-washed
building perches over the sea
on the promenade. Mid-priced
fish and a few meat dishes are
always fresh, or pop into the bar
opposite, hewn into the volcanic
rock.

Dona Amélia

Rua Imperatriz D. Amélia 83 ☎291 225
784. Daily 12.30–3pm & 7–11pm. An
attractive, traditional building
lined with hanging plants and
azulejos; there is also a basement
bar. The meat is hit or miss, but
the seafood and pasta are usually
good and reasonably priced,
as are the speciality flambés.
Desserts include *kebab de frutos*
tropicais. Main courses from
around €13.

Les Faunes

Reid's Palace Hotel, Estrada
Monumental 139 ☎291 717 171.
Oct–May Tues–Sat 7–9.30pm; closed
rest of year. Reservations essential.
The ultimate in French *haute
cuisine* – with a few oriental
and Madeiran influences – in a
plush restaurant tucked into a
corner of *Reid's Hotel*. Original
Picassos on the wall vie with
the harbour views for your
attention. You may find yourself
rubbing shoulders with visiting
celebs, and you'll need to check
your bank balance carefully
before you pay. Dress is smart.

Lido Mar

Rua do Gorgulho-Lido ☎291 764 369.
Daily noon–3pm & 6–11pm. The lido
restaurant, which you can eat
in even if you're not using the
lido facilities, is very good, set
in an attractive spot overlooking
the sea and the pools below.
The long menu offers a wide
range of dishes from around
€12, including *arroz de tamboril*
(monkfish rice) and *bacalhau*.

Moby Dick

Estrada Monumental 187 ☎291
776 868. Mon–Sat 11am–midnight.
Despite its location in a dull
forecourt of a modern block,
this is actually a very good
restaurant. The interior is
pleasantly traditional, while the
specialities include excellent
seafood dishes such as *gambas
piri piri* (spicy prawns), a few
vegetarian options and what
some people consider to be
the best fresh fish in Funchal.
The owner will pick up clients
from their hotel in his minibus
(minimum of four people if you
are not staying nearby). Fresh
fish starts at €8.

PLACES Western Funchal and the Hotel Zone

O Molhe

Estrada da Pontinha, Forte de Nossa Senhora da Conceiçao ☎291 203 848. Mon–Sat 7pm–11pm. A spectacularly positioned restaurant right on top of the rocky fort on Loo Rock, jutting out of the city harbour walls, and reached by a lift. The glass-walled restaurant offers 360-degree views over the sea, the city and the mountains beyond. The menu features *bodião* (parrot fish), lamb with couscous and other meat and seafood, with mains from around €13. Reservations advised at weekends.

Paradise

Estrada Monumental 179 ☎291 762 559. Daily 10am–midnight. Run by the tourism association, with its own seawater swimming pools and on a sun terrace below the cliffs, *Paradise* has an idyllic position facing the sea. Service is swift and the Madeiran and Portuguese cuisine is good and well priced. Dishes include *leitão*

(roast suckling pig), *pato* (duck) and the usual fish dishes.

Bars

Bar da Cidade

Avenida do Infante ☎291 220 292. Daily 8pm–4am. A lively Brazilian music bar, with boppy sounds and a happy crowd, though be prepared for the scantily clad dancing girls.

Casino da Madeira

Avenida do Infante ☎291 209 180. Daily 8pm–4am. Predictably over-the-top, glitzy and generally naff floor shows add to the serious business of card playing and chucking money into slot machines. However, the in-house disco, Copacabana, in the basement can be fun, and often hosts special events and shows, especially at Christmas.

Fórmula 1

Rua da Favila 5 ☎291 775 755. Daily 10pm–6am. A popular music bar

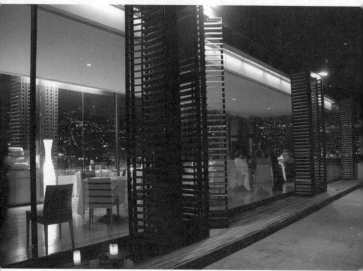

▲ O MOLHE

that attracts a boisterous late-night crowd; stays open way after the others on this stretch.

Glória Latina

Rua Imperatriz Dona Amélia 101 ☎291 282 266. Mon–Sat noon–2am. With wooden floors and subtle lighting, this modern bar has a sophisticated feel, and gets particularly animated with the live Latin music most weekends.

Harry's Bar

Rua Imperatriz Dona Amélia 69 ☎291 205 600. Daily 12.30pm–midnight. An English-style pub with a lovely patio filled with plants and *azulejos*; the sign outside just says *The Pub*. Live piano music most nights.

O Molhe

Estrada da Pontinha, Forte de Nossa Senhora da Conceição ☎291 203 840. Café and bar daily 3pm–midnight; club Fri & Sat midnight–6am. A superbly positioned café-bar right at the top of Loo Rock, reached by a lift. The sea views are exhilarating and the prices not too outrageous. At weekends, it becomes a great club from midnight onwards, with house and dance music in one room and rock in the other; entry charge around €5.

Pub No. 2

Rua da Favila 2 ☎291 230 276. Daily 11am–2am. An unoriginal name but a charismatic, low-ceilinged bar comprising two wood-panelled rooms hung with agricultural implements. There's a small outside terrace, live soccer on the TV and a healthy mix of locals and tourists of all ages.

www.cyber Café

Avenida Infante 6 ☎291 236 948. Mon–Sat 8am–1am. Not just a cyber-café, but a lively student bar in its own right, with either MTV or Sports TV and a permanent buzz.

Clubs

Jam

Avda Sá Carneiro 60 ☎291 234 800. Fri & Sat midnight–6am. An intimate disco attracting a retro crowd not embarrassed to get down to Gary Glitter, Abba and the likes.

Marginal

Avenida Sá Carneiro ☎291 234 800. Fri & Sat midnight–6am. Facing the harbour, this is one of the smallest but most popular of the trio of clubs on this stretch. Alternative and deep house music rule the roost, with a high-energy, youthful clientele.

Vespas

Avenida Sá Carneiro 60 ☎291 234 800, 🌐www.discotecavespas.com. Wed (Ladies' night) midnight–5.30am, Fri & Sat midnight–7am. Funchal's best-known nightclub, set in a suitably gritty-looking former warehouse opposite the entrance to the harbour. The music is basically club and house, with pounding rhythms and a spectacular light show. The atmosphere is friendly, as long as you don't object to the mainly young crowd dancing on the speakers. The minimum consumption policy of €125 a head isn't always adhered to, but be prepared.

Eastern Funchal and the Old Town

The area immediately east of the centre of Funchal is largely given over to bustling shopping streets, but it does contain a couple of notable sights: the engaging handicrafts museum IBTAM and the Museu de Franco, dedicated to the works of two local artists. Further east, the Mercado dos Lavradores, the central market, is one of Funchal's most characterful spots, and marks the beginning of the Zona Velha, or Old Town, with its bars, restaurants and atmospheric cobbled streets clustered round a seafront fort. Steeply uphill lie three superb gardens.

Praça do Carmo

Praça do Carmo is an attractive square full of outdoor café tables and surrounded by a warren of narrow pedestrianzed shopping streets. It takes its name from the pretty Igreja do Carmo, an eighteenth-century Baroque church, containing some fine *azulejos* and the tomb of the Conde de Carvalhal, the original owner of Quinta Palheiro Ferreiro (see p.100).

Museu de Henrique e Francisco Franco

Rua de João de Deus. Mon–Fri 10am–12.30pm & 2–6pm. €1.70.
Set in a 1940s building, the Museu de Henrique e Francisco Franco is dedicated to two of Madeira's most important modern artists, surprisingly little known internationally. The more famous of the two brothers, Franco, was born in Funchal in 1885 and his Monument to João Gonçalves Zarco graces Avenida Arriaga in the centre of Funchal. His career took off after he exhibited with Picasso in Boston in 1927, when his work attracted the attention of Portugal's dictator Salazar. Salazar commissioned Franco to create statues of great Portuguese heroes and, of course, himself. Many of these works are now in mainland Portugal, though a number are on display here, including the powerful *Torso de Mulher* ("Body of a woman", 1922), heavily influenced by Rodin. What is most impressive about Franco's works is his wide

▼ MUSEU DE HENRIQUE E FRANCISCO FRANCO

▲ MERCADO DOS LAVRADORES

museum and the varied exhibits and photographs give some insight into the importance of crafts to the island's art and culture. Perhaps the most interesting exhibit – if only for its size – is an enormous tapestry entitled *Allegory of Madeira*, hung in the main hallway, halfway up the stairs. It took over three years to complete, from 1958 to 1961. Other highlights include an Irish linen cloth embroidered by Madeirans for Queen Elizabeth II's visit to Lisbon in 1957 and a bedchamber as it would have looked in the nineteenth century.

Mercado dos Lavradores

Main entrance on Largo dos Lavradores. Mon–Thurs 7am–4pm, Fri 7am–8pm, Sat 7am–2pm. Funchal's vibrant main market, the Mercado dos Lavradores, sells a colourful array of fish, exotic fruits and local crafts. Housed in a yellow building faced with *azulejos*, it was designed in the 1930s by Edmundo Tavares, one of Portugal's best-known twentieth-century architects. Much of its appeal lies in the theatrical air lent by the tiers of arcades, thronged with shoppers looking down on the activity in the central courtyard below. The lower tier contains counter after counter of scabbard fish, vast octopi, tuna steaks the size of frisbees and other weird-looking Atlantic fish. The main ground-floor area is a medley of stalls selling vegetables, exotic fruit and wickerwork. The upper floor has more fruit and vegetables, along with dried chillies, clothes and caged birds.

Museu de Electricidade

Rua da Casa da Luz 2. Tues–Sat 10am–12.30pm & 2–6pm. €2.

range of styles, from classical to modern – see for example his tile designs and black and white pencil sketches; look out, too, for the evocative, minimalist *Cena do Café* ("Scene in a café", 1923). The museum also contains works by Franco's brother, Henriques, a highly respected painter in his own right, known for his portrayal of scenes from Madeiran everyday life.

IBTAM

Rua do Visconde de Anadia 44. Mon–Fri 10am–12.30pm & 2.30–5.30pm. €2. The Instituto de Bordados Tapeçaria e Artesanato de Madeira (Institute of Embroidery, Tapestry and Craftsmanship of Madeira), or IBTAM, was set up in 1978 to monitor standards of Madeira's longstanding handicrafts industry and provide training. The tradition of embroidery, in particular, goes back a long way, a continuation of a skill practised in Portuguese convents since the Middle Ages. The upper floor is now a handicrafts

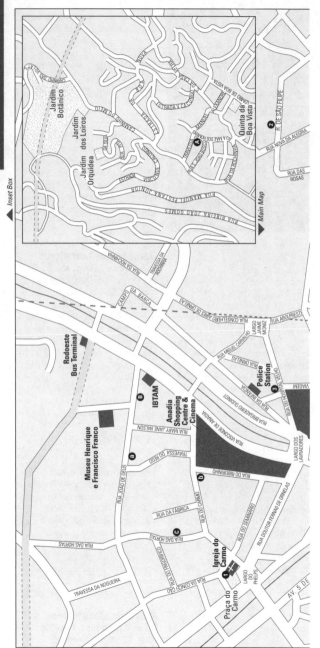

Inset Box

Jardim Botânico
Jardim dos Loiros
Jardim Orquídea

Quinta da Boa Vista

Main Map

Rodoeste Bus Terminal

IBTAM

Anadia Shopping Centre & Cinema

Museu Henrique e Francisco Franco

Police Station

Igreja do Carmo

Praça do Carmo

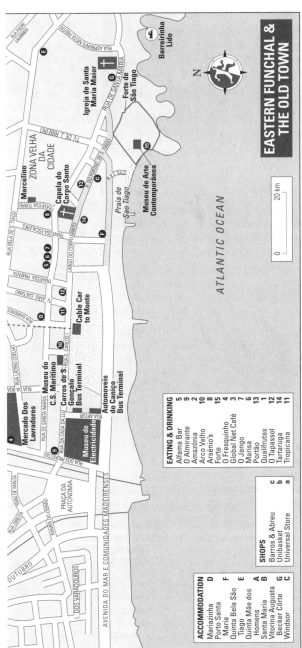

**EASTERN FUNCHAL &
THE OLD TOWN**

N

ATLANTIC OCEAN

0   20 km

EATING & DRINKING

Alfama Bar	5
O Almirante	9
Amazónia	2
Arco Velho	10
Arsénio's	8
Forte	15
O Fresquinho	4
Global Net Café	3
O Jango	7
Marisa	6
Portão	13
Qualifrutas	1
O Tapassol	12
Tartaruga	14
Tropicana	11

SHOPS

Barros & Abreu	c
Unibasket	b
Universal Store	a

ACCOMMODATION

Mariazinha	D
Porto Santa Maria	F
Quinta Bela São Tiago	E
Quinta Mãe dos Homens	A
Santa Maria	B
Vitorina Augusta	G
Becker Côrte	C
Windsor	

AVENIDA DO MAR E COMUNIDADES MADEIRENSES

▲ FORTE DE SÃO TIAGO

Set in the high-ceilinged, former Central Power Station of Funchal, the Museu de Electricidade is a surprisingly engaging museum charting the history of electricity and lighting in Madeira and illustrated with dials, generators, photos, illustrations and real street lamps. You learn that the British ran the first electricity supply in 1897 (it was not until the end of the World War II that power was literally in the hands of the local council) and how during the war, electricity shortages made it necessary to develop water-powered generators, leading to HEP in the 1950s, still one of the primary sources of energy on the island today.

Museu do Club Sport Marítimo

Rua Dom Carlos 14. Mon–Fri 9am–noon & 2–7pm. Free. The Museu do Club Sport Marítimo is dedicated to the exploits of the city's most successful soccer team (see p.200). You can also buy tickets for matches at the downstairs desk. The upstairs room is full of trophies, pennants and photographs, with pride of place given to the cup that the team won for the 1925–26 Portuguese Championship.

The cable car to Monte

Daily: May–Sept 10am–8.30pm; Oct–April 10am–6pm. €9 single, €14 return; children half price.

The high-tech cable car to Monte (see p.93) is a feat of engineering, its glass bubbles swaying between huge green metal pillars erected amid Funchal's buildings. The ten-minute ride is exhilarating.

Old Town

The Old Town, or Zona Velha, is an atmospheric area of cobbled streets, dotted with flowering mimosa trees and lined with former fishermen's houses, some dating back to the first colonization of Funchal in the fifteenth century. Though it's filled with restaurants firmly geared to tourists, its population is still predominantly working class; in the evenings, locals chat on the doosteps and children play in the street.

The focal point of the area is Largo do Corpo Santo, on one side of which sits the small Capela do Corpo Santo, believed to be one of the oldest chapels on the island, dating from the sixteenth century, and dedicated to São Pedro, the patron saint of fishermen.

Forte de São Tiago and the Museu de Arte Contemporânea

Mon–Sat 10am–12.30pm & 2–5.30pm. €2. Set on a little rocky outcrop overlooking the sea is the **Forte de São Tiago** with its distinctive ochre walls. Built in 1614 to defend the city from pirate attack, the structure later became what must have been a cramped home to 3500 British troops, stationed in Funchal during the Napoleonic wars. Britain was keen to protect its commercial interests in Madeira from the French, who briefly occupied mainland Portugal before the British pushed them back. In 1803, the fort was again occupied when it became a temporary shelter to the thousands of locals made homeless by the devastating floods which hit the capital. It now houses a couple of small and rather uninspiring museums, though it is worth the admission price just to wander round its rambling ramparts.

Overlooking the courtyard is the **Military Room**, containing a tiny, rather dull collection of military maps, illustrations and weapons. You're better off following the arrows to the former military governor's house, which since 1992 has been occupied by the **Museu de Arte Contemporânea**, a rather hit-and-miss collection of contemporary Portuguese art from 1960 to the present. Highlights include some interesting photographic works by Helena Almeida (1971) on the top floor, and some attractive work by Pedro Cabrita Ries, notably *Naturália Parte 6* (1996), along with Rui Sanches' cracked tile effects in pale blue and white on the floor below. The bottom floor displays some colourful works by Eduardo de Freitas, one of the few Madeiran artists on show.

Praia de São Tiago

Just by the entrance to the fort, Rua Portão São Tiago leads to the Praia de São Tiago, a little stony beach. Locals swim off it in summer, and use the concrete terrace behind for sunbathing.

There is also a tiny seasonal kiosk café serving cold beers.

The Barreirinha Lido

Daily 9am–6pm. €1, extra charges for use of chairs and sun umbrellas. Bus #40 from Avenida do Mar. Set under the cliffs is the modest Barreirinha Lido, comprising a gym, changing rooms and a seawater pool, just about deep enough to submerge yourself in and certainly great for kids. You can also swim off a small stony beach.

Igreja de Santa Maria Maior

Rua de Santa Maria. The Baroque seventeenth-century Igreja de Santa Maria Maior is one of the most attractive churches in the city. Also known as Igreja de São Tiago or Socorro, the church was built on the site of an earlier chapel constructed to commemorate the plague of 1538. There is still a procession every May 1 in honour of the plague victims.

Jardim Botânico and Museu de História Natural

Caminho do Meio. Daily 9am–6pm. €3, valid for Loiro Parque (see below). Buses #29 and #30 from Largo dos Lavradores/Rua da Infância or #31 from opposite the marina. The Jardim Botânico consists of a series of lawns, woods and grottoes, ideal for a walk or a picnic. Furthermore, the views back over the city make it an unmissable spot. The grounds were once part of a private estate, the Quinta do Bom Successo, owned by the Reid family (see p.72), who laid out the gardens as a private park. The gardens contain some 2000 exotic plant species from five continents, including papyrus grass, anthurium and bird-of-paradise – although most plants are either indigenous or from the Azores, Cape Verde or the Canaries.

Close to the park entrance is the **Museu de História Natural** (daily 9am–5.30pm), a rather quaint collection of pickled fish, dusty stuffed birds, mammals and fossils, collected from round the island. The highlight is a giant, ten-million-year-old fossilized tree heather, found in an underground cavern that was discovered during tunnelling for one of Madeira's new roads; the cavern was found to be full of similar fossils, but most have been left *in situ*.

Nearby is the garden's café, a bit pricey, but boasting superb views. Below the museum lies an extraordinary collection of cacti and succulents, ranging from tiny, flowering cacti to enormous spiky ones, their spines draped in cobwebs.

Loiro Parque

Hours and entry as Jardim Botânico (see above). Entered from the Botanical Gardens, or via a separate entrance on Caminho do Meio, the Loiro Parque bird garden has a colourful array of tropical birds, including macaws, green and crimson parakeets and salmon-crested cockatoos. Children will particularly enjoy chasing the peacocks which roam about at will, or stumbling across the giant tortoise.

Jardim Orquídea

Rua Pita da Silva 37. Daily 9am–6pm. €5. Buses #29 and #30 from Largo dos Lavradores/Rua da Infância or #31 from opposite the marina. The Jardim Orquídea (orchid farm) contains some 50,000 plants representing around 4000 varieties of orchid. The main flowering season is from November to April, though there are usually some species in bloom at other times. True orchid-philes can find out about the technicalities of the flower's cultivation, explained here in great detail. If you want to buy a plant (packaged in easily transportable glass jars), those suitable for growing in colder climates are well labelled.

Quinta da Boa Vista

Rua Lombo da Boa Vista 25. Mon–Sat 9am–5.30pm. €2.50. Take bus #32 from Avenida do Mar to the end of the line, then it's a five-minute walk downhill. The attractive eighteenth-century Quinta Boa Vista is owned by the former Honorary British Consul to Madeira and contains one of Madeira's most important collections of orchids, featuring many rare species. Covered areas under green gauze shelter row upon row of potted orchids in a spectacular range of shapes and colours. It's best to come early, as it can get crowded. Just below the orchid houses there is a lovely lawned area set out with tables and chairs, where tea and cake are sometimes served.

▲ JARDIM BOTÁNICO

Hotels

Residencial da Mariazinha

Rua de Santa Maria 155 ☎291 220 239, ⊛www.residencialmariazinha.com. In the heart of the Zona Velha, this beautifully renovated town house has good-sized rooms decked out in contemporary style. There's also a large breakfast room. €70.

Hotel Porto Santa Maria

Avenida do Mar 50 ☎291 206 700, ⊛www.portobay.com. Superbly positioned modern four-star on the edge of the old town, facing the sea. Rooms are functional but spacious – all have kitchenettes and the best ones face the waves. A large outdoor area includes a small pool and bar, and breakfast can be taken on the terrace. There's also an indoor pool, sauna and gym. The in-house restaurant, *Arsenal*, serves, as you'd expect from the name, international fare with aplomb. €142.

Quinta Bela São Tiago

Rua Bela São Tiago 70 ☎291 204 500, ⊛www.hotel-qta-bela-s-tiago .com. Built in 1894, this stunning *quinta* has been tastefully extended with two modern wings just a stone's throw from the Zona Velha. Most rooms have balconies facing the spires of the old town and the sea. There's also a pool, terrace and small garden, along with a gym, sauna, jacuzzi, restaurant and bar, a great place to watch the sun set. €155.

Quinta Mãe dos Homens

Rua Mãe dos Homens 39 ☎291 204 410, ⊛www.qmdh.com. A small complex of spotless, roomy self-catering studios and apartments set behind an old *quinta* amidst

▲ ORCHIDS AT QUINTA DA BOA VISTA

a mini banana plantation in the attractive residential suburb of Rochinha, close to the botanical gardens. There's a pool, honesty bar and weekly barbecue evenings. The only drawback is the steep fifteen-minute climb uphill from the centre, though its lofty position commands great vistas. Breakfast not included. €100.

Hotel Santa Maria

Rua João de Deus 26 ☎291 225 271, ⊛www.maisturismo.pt/hstmaria. A largish three-star hotel, close to IBTAM and the market. Rooms are reasonably sized, some with balconies, and all come with TVs and bathrooms. There's a restaurant with live entertainment twice weekly, a games room and a small rooftop pool with views of the harbour in the distance. €65.

Vitorina Augusta Becker Côrte

Rua de Santa Maria 279 ☎291 220 249. An unsigned, extremely characterful family house near the Barreirinha Lido. Rooms come in an array of sizes, the

PLACES Eastern Funchal and the Old Town

cheapest ones with shared bathrooms; all are clean, airy and simply furnished, with electric coffee-makers the only touch of sophistication. There's an apartment with a kitchenette on the ground floor (€40), but the upper rooms are most appealing. The best room is the "tower" room jutting out from the roof, with its own shower and small covered terrace facing the sea. Breakfast not included. €30.

Hotel Windsor

Rua das Hortas 4C ☎291 233 081, ⊕www.hotelwindsorgroup.pt. A neo-Art Deco block with unevenly shaped rooms, none of which is particularly big, but it has a friendly atmosphere and a small café and restaurant downstairs. There's also a rooftop pool. €66.

Shops

Barros & Abreu Irmãos Peles e Botas

Rua do Portão de São Tiago 22–23. Mon–Fri 9am–1pm & 3–7pm, Sat 9am–1pm. A traditional family workshop where typical

Madeiran *cordovo* (goatskin boots) are made to measure on the premises at very reasonable rates.

Unibasket

Rua do Carmo 44. Mon–Fri 10am–1pm & 2–7pm, Sat 10am–1pm. A large store with a big yard out back stashed with quality household goods from Madeira and the east, including ceramics, statues, furniture and a large range of wicker chairs and baskets.

Universal Store

Rua de João de Deus 14a. Daily 9.30am–7.30pm. Handicrafts emporium set in a former Protestant church. Prices aren't particularly cheap but it offers a wide range of goods including embroidery, leather belts, pottery, *azulejos*, clothes and children's toys, while the basement is stuffed with an enormous selection of wines.

Cafés

Arco Velho

Rua Dom Carlos I 42. Daily 8am–midnight. Lively café, especially busy on a Sunday morning when locals gather here to read the Sunday papers over coffee and drinks. There's an outdoor terrace from where you can watch the capsules pass overhead on the Funchal–Monte cable car. The small *pastelaria* section does a decent range of pastries, and its main meals are also good value.

▲ RUA DE SANTA MARIA

O Fresquinho

Mercado dos Lavradores. Mon–Fri 8am–8pm, Sat 8am–2pm. The most appealing of the market's café-bars, set in the front of the upper floor with a stand-up bar area and a few tables set to the side surrounded by plants and hemmed in by stalls selling fruit and plucked chickens. Sells sandwiches, snacks, beers and coffee.

Global Net Café

Rua Hospital Velho 25. Mon–Fri 9am–7pm, Sat 9am–2am. Fashionable little cyber café opposite the market, with two terminals and fine coffee.

Qualifrutas

Praça do Carmo. Mon–Sat 8am–8pm. Fruit shop which doubles as a café specializing in fruit and milkshakes, along with cakes and sandwiches; there's upstairs seating or, best of all, outdoor tables under the arcades of the attractive square.

Restaurants

O Almirante

Largo do Poço 1–2 ☏291 224 252. Daily 8am–midnight. The beautiful first-floor dining room features wood beams, chandeliers and high-backed chairs – it's a lovely spot to enjoy *bacalhau* and other fish, lobster, squid, kebabs and dishes such as *Fidago ao Madeira* (Madeiran liver). There's also a good *pastelaria* section downstairs. Mains from €12.

Arsénio's

Rua da Santa Maria 169 ☏291 224 007. Daily 7pm–midnight. Highly rated for its fish and meat dishes, with an outdoor grill wafting mouth-watering smells to the tables under the covered porch.

Most people head here for the nightly fado sessions in the *azulejos*-lined interior, which bumps up the prices, but at least the fado is more authentic than the cheesy warm-up musicians on electric keyboards. It's one of the old town's most popular dining spots so get there early or book ahead.

Restaurante do Forte

Forte de São Tiago, Rua Portão de São Tiago ☏291 235 740. Daily noon–3pm & 6.30–11pm. A smart little restaurant inside the fort, sometimes booked for wedding receptions, with outdoor tables facing the sea. International dishes – pasta, salads, meat and fish – along with great soufflés and crepes for dessert. Mains start at €13, though diners do get free entry to the museums.

O Jango

Rua de Santa Maria 166 ☏291 221 280. Daily 11am–11pm. Small split-level restaurant crammed into a former fisherman's house with a reputation for excellent-value food. Stick to the simple grilled fish dishes and the reputation is justified; other dishes tend to be smothered in rich sauces and served with over-boiled vegetables. Clam *cataplana, gambas a Indiana* (Indian-style prawns) and the house wine are also good. Mains from €12.

Marisa

Rua de Santa Maria 162 ☏291 226 189. Daily 11am–11pm. An attractive, family-run restaurant with traditional decor and upstairs seating on a small interior balcony. Specialities include *paella, arroz de marisco* (seafood rice) and prawns with chilli, and, with advance notice, *cabrito* (goat) and *leitão* (suckling pig). It's pretty tiny, so booking is advisable. Mains from €8.

Portão
Rua do Portão de São Tiago ⑦291 221 125. Fri–Wed noon–midnight. This restaurant has outdoor tables and an attractive interior, decorated with mock wood beams and *azulejos*. Service is friendly and unpretentious and the fish, meat and the *bacalhau* dishes are, at around €10, good value.

O Tapassol
Rua Dom Carlos I 62 ⑦291 225 023. Daily 11am–11pm. Very good quality, if pricey, Portuguese staples. Its other attraction is an upstairs terrace offering sea views. Gets booked up, so ring in advance or turn up early.

Tartaruga
Largo do Corpo Santo 4–6 ⑦291 280 645. Daily 10am–midnight. A tiny place with a couple of tables wedged inside and more spreading onto the attractive square. Serves a hybrid of very inexpensive Portuguese and British dishes to a non-local

clientele. The place to go if you hanker for sausages, beans, eggs and the like, though the Portuguese-oriented set meals are perhaps the best value.

Marisqueira Tropicana
Rua Dom Carlos I 43 ⑦291 225 705. Daily 10am–1pm. More reasonably priced than many of the restaurants on this unpedestrianized stretch of Rua Dom Carlos, with good-value tuna, fish and Portuguese dishes. There's also a pleasant street-facing terrace.

Bars

Alfama Bar
Rua da Santa Maria 160. Mon–Sat 8am–midnight, Sun 6pm–midnight. Recently renovatd, this cosy, darkened bar has a stone arched ceiling and wooden bench-like seats – a good night-time drinks spot in the heart of the Zona Velha.

Amazónia
Rua de São Felipe 19. Daily 4pm–2am. Very popular with a young crowd, this friendly bar has tropical decor and thumping music. Musical volume is diminished in a lovely garden, a great spot to nurse a drink or two.

Live music

Marcelino
Travessa das Torres 22a ⑦291 220 216. Daily 10pm–2am. Set in a low-ceilinged traditional building, this fado house is the best place in town to sample the traditional Portuguese version of the blues.

▲ THE DAY'S CATCH AT MARISA

Monte and northeast of Funchal

One of the easiest and most rewarding half-day trips from Funchal is to Monte, a hilltop town overlooking the capital and site of some spectacular gardens. Getting to and from Monte is half the fun: up on the cable car and down on an exhilarating dry toboggan run. To the east lie the Balancal golf course and Quinta do Palheiro Ferreiro – more popularly known as Blandy's – a must for garden lovers, with a riot of tropical plants set in extensive grounds. All these places are accessible by public transport, but are also connected by paths and the Levada dos Tornos, which makes a gentle introduction to Madeira's spectacular walks.

Monte

Funchal city buses #20 and #21, from Praça da Autonomia, and #48, from the Hotel Zone (every 10min); also by cable car from the Zona Velha (see p.86). The attractive hilltop town of Monte perches 550m above sea level and is a six-kilometre climb northeast of Funchal. Its wooded slopes, cool air and dramatic views established it in the mid-nineteenth century as a healthy retreat for the island's wealthy residents and as a popular base for transatlantic passengers stopping off in Madeira. Numerous *quintas* were built in and around the town to put visitors up before the first hotel appeared in Funchal at the end of the nineteenth century. In 1893, a rack-and-pinion railway was constructed to serve the town, terminating at Terreiro da Luta (see p.98). Unfortunately, the steam-boilers that powered the trains proved alarmingly prone to exploding – four people were killed in one explosion in 1919 – and though the service struggled

on until 1939, people lost faith in its safety and it was finally discontinued. After World War II,

▲ THE CABLE CAR TO MONTE

Monte's fortunes diminished as Funchal took over as the main centre for tourism, though it has remained one of the most popular excursions from the capital. Most visitors arrive by the cable car (see p.86), which terminates at Caminho das Barbosas, by one of the entrances to the Jardins Tropicais do Monte Palace (see p.96); to reach the main square, Largo da Fonte, turn left and continue down Caminho das Barbosas for around 200m.

Buses from Funchal stop on Largo da Fonte, centred on a little bandstand, overlooking the verdant Parque do Monte public gardens, which spread down the gully below. The park is bordered to the east by parts of the old viaduct of the defunct rack-and-pinion railway, whose arches are covered in vegetation. To the east of the square is

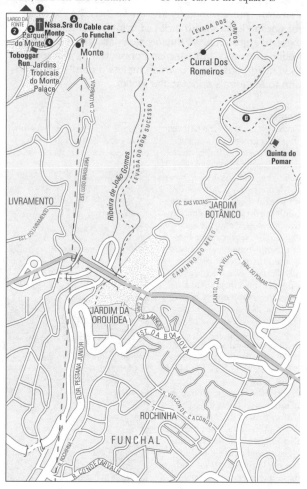

the Fonte da Virgem, a little fountain with a shrine to Nossa Senhora do Monte.

Monte: Nossa Senhora do Monte

The twin-towered Nossa Senhora do Monte (Our Lady of the Mountain) is the island's most important church and stands on the site of one of Madeira's first chapels, built in 1470 by Adam Gonçalves Ferreira, one of a pair of twins (his sister was called Eve) who, appropriately enough, were the first children born on the island. The original chapel was levelled in the 1748 earthquake and was replaced by the current Baroque structure in 1818, an attractive building with low-hanging chandeliers and a painted ceiling.

The church altar displays a particularly revered tiny

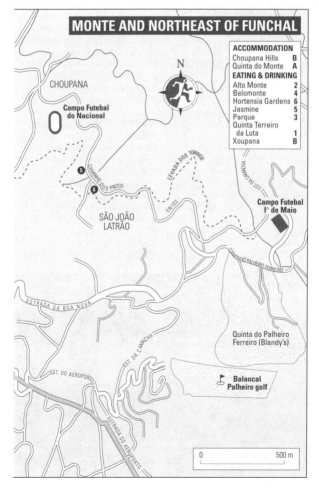

▲ NOSSA SENHORA DO MONTE

statue of the Virgin, found by a shepherdess in nearby Terreira da Luta (see p.98) in the fifteenth century; *azulejos* panels on the front of the church depict the moment of discovery. During the Feast of Assumption on August 14–15, pilgrims climb the church's 74 rough basalt steps on their knees to pay homage to the Virgin – a feat which looks as painful as it sounds – before the statue is taken out and processed. Far less solemn is the *romaria* in the evening, a festival with music and fireworks.

The church is also the final resting place of Emperor Karl I of Austria and King of Hungary, the last Hapsburg monarch, who was deposed in 1918 at the end of World War I after just two years in power. In 2004, he was sanctified by the Pope for his efforts to end the war. Karl was married to Princess Zita, the granddaughter of Dom Miguel I of Portugal, and when in 1921 the emperor was banished from his homeland, he came to Madeira with Zita in the hope that the warm climate would improve his health. He first stayed at *Reid's* before moving to the Quinta Gordon in Monte. He died of pneumonia, however, a year later, aged 35. His tomb is on the left of the altar in a rather spartan side room.

Jardins Tropicais do Monte Palace

Caminho do Monte 174 ⊛www
.montepalace.com. Mon–Sat
9.30am–6pm. €10. If you visit just one garden on Madeira, you should make it the Jardins Tropicais do Monte Palace, as much a museum as a garden, filled with fountains, statues and works of art, as well as a spectacular range of plants. The

▲ JARDINS TROPICAIS DO MONTE PALACE

gardens spill down seventeen acres of verdant ravine towards the eighteenth-century building that is home to the park's owner, José Rodrigues Berardo, a local tobacco magnate and one of Portugal's leading arts benefactors. As well as setting up the park's imaginative range of exhibits, he has introduced to the gardens rare cycads – prehistoric tree ferns (cicas) from South Africa (there are now more examples of this species here than anywhere else in the world) – azaleas and heathers from northern Europe and indigenous plants from Madeira.

The park entrance lies above an **Art and Minerals Museum** (daily 10.30am–3.30pm), displaying petrified wood, African stone carvings and around a thousand semi-precious stones from around the world. From the entrance, paths descend past koi fish ponds down a series of steps into the ravine. One path is lined with decorative modern *azulejos* panels, each showing key moments in Portugal's history – the most dramatic is the one of the Great Earthquake in Lisbon in 1755, which is followed by a series showing the rebuilding of the capital. Just beyond here, a formal Japanese-style garden shelters 166 colourful glazed panels tracing the 450-year trading alliance between Portugal and Japan.

Further down the slope spectacular plants form the backdrop to large, flamboyant stone Manueline doors, dating back to the Golden Age of Portuguese navigation. Near the doors, just in front of the park's main lake, you can't miss the world's largest ceramic vase, which stands 5.345m high and

▲ PREPARING THE TOBOGGAN RUN

weighs 555 kilos. Southeast of the lake, a path leads down to the park café.

Monte: the toboggan run

Carreiros do Monte. Mon–Sat 9am–6pm, Sun 9am–1pm. €10 per person for the 10min ride to Livramento; minimum of two people. For most people, the toboggan run is the most memorable experience to be had in Monte. You'll see the dapper-looking drivers lined up on the street beneath the church in pristine white trousers and shirts, with straw boaters and goatskin boots. The toboggans are basically giant wicker baskets, known as *carros de cesto* (basket cars), attached to wooden runners, which are oiled using a greasy rag. Until the mid-nineteenth century, similar baskets were pulled up and down the slopes by horses and bullocks, but in 1850 they were adapted so that two drivers could control their descent to transport produce to the town's market, as well as carrying local landowners. They quickly became popular with visiting tourists, and Ernest Hemingway, who had his fair share of adventures, described the ride as one of the most exhilarating experiences in his life.

Today this means of transport continues for tourists alone. The drivers seat you in the baskets, then get you going with the aid of ropes, hopping onto the back as you pick up speed. It can be pretty scary as you plummet downhill, though in fact you are not going as fast as it feels, and the baskets are easily stopped: the drivers' goatskin boots have special rubber-treaded soles that act as brakes. The baskets are manoeuvred over manhole covers and past potholes in the road; the most alarming bit is when occasionally the sleds start to veer off at an angle, a sign that the runners need extra oil.

Rides end up a couple of kilometres downhill in the suburb of Livramento, where there are a couple of cafés,

a bus stop and usually a taxi waiting to take people back into Funchal.

Terreiro da Luta

São Gonçalo bus #103 from Monte (2 daily); or bus #138 (1 daily, not Sun), or #56 (Mon–Fri 2 daily, Sun 1 daily). The impressive hillside monument of Terreiro da Luta marks the spot where a local shepherdess found the statue of the Virgin, now in Nossa Senhora do Monte (see p.95). Composed of an elaborate stone column supporting a statue of the Virgin, the monument was built in 1927 as a memorial to the end of World War I. At the height of the war in 1916, Madeira came under attack from German submarines, during which a French ship was hit, killing several people. The Madeirans prayed at the altar of the church in Monte and vowed to build the statue if the war was stopped. This they duly did and today, at the foot of

A walk from Monte to the Jardim Botânico

This walk, taking between an hour and a half and two hours, is a relatively gentle one along footpaths, a *levada* and steep roads, and offers superb views over Funchal en route. It covers parts of the Levada dos Tornos walk from Quinta do Palheiro Ferreiro detailed in the opposite direction on p.100.

From Monte, head past the entrance to the cable car and continue straight on at a turning point by Barbosas church. You'll pick up the track signed Curral dos Romeiros. A cobbled path takes you down, round and up a wooded steep valley, and in thirty minutes you'll arrive in the little village of Curral dos Romeiros. Head through the village on the main track, and you'll see steps on the left signed Levada dos Tornos/Camacha. Take these and follow the *levada* path, which winds through eucalyptus woods; after around thirty minutes you'll pass the log cabins of the *Choupana Hills* resort. Continue along the *levada* and in another ten minutes you'll reach a road. Turn right and head steeply downhill. The main road veers left after 150m or so, but carry on down a very steep, semi-stepped cobbled track. After five minutes you'll reach a junction with two restaurants on your right. If you have strong knees, you can continue straight on down the steep Caminho do Meio, which will bring you out in front of the Botanical Gardens (see p.87) after another five to ten minutes. Alternatively, turn right at the junction along the busier Caminho das Voltas, which winds more gently downhill – bus #29 (two hourly) passes along this stretch on its way into Funchal – and after twenty minutes you'll come out by the Botanical Gardens' entrance.

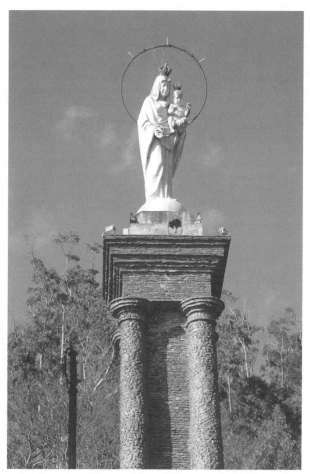

▲ TERREIRO DA LUTA MONUMENT

the statue, you can still see the anchor chains from the French ship that was destroyed in the bombardment.

By the road junction near the statue is the old terminus of the short-lived Funchal–Monte railway line; the defunct station building, dating from 1912, is now a restaurant (see p.103).

It's a steep climb to get to Terreiro da Luta, so if you don't have a car it's best to take a bus (ask for Terreiro da Luta and you'll be dropped 200m or so from the statue) or a taxi (around €5 one-way), but the walk back down to Monte is well worth doing. Take the steep cobbled track next to the old station building, heading downhill past stations of the cross, with a distant Funchal as a backdrop. Yellow and red markers direct you along the Caminha das Laginhas – past traditional village houses – and onto the Caminho do Monte in Monte, around twenty minutes' walk.

Quinta do Palheiro Ferreiro (Blandy's)

Mon–Fri 9am–noon & 2–5pm. €7. Horários do Funchal city bus #36 (14 daily) or #37 (Mon–Fri 7 daily, Sat & Sun 5 daily) from Praça da Autonomia. Better known as Blandy's, the estate of Quinta do Palheiro Ferreiro is a must if you like formal gardens. The thirty-acre estate was founded by the Portuguese Count of Carvalhal in the early nineteenth century, when a *quinta* and the Baroque chapel were built in the middle of formal gardens and the grounds stocked with deer. Later, during the Miguelite uprising, the Count was forced to flee Madeira for England,

and when he returned to the island, he introduced some of the gardening techniques he had encountered there – at 550m in altitude, the cool climate is similar to Britain's, allowing trees such as oaks, beech and chestnuts to thrive. He also introduced ornamental ponds and planted camellia trees as wind breaks – these produce vivid red flowers from December to around April and are now one of the garden's highlights.

In 1884 the estate was bought out by the powerful Blandy family, who had settled in Madeira after the Napoleonic wars and stayed on to set up Blandy's Madeira Wine Company in Funchal. The Blandys established their family home here and added plants from round the world,

A walk from Quinta do Palheiro Ferreiro to Monte

From Quinta do Palheiro Ferreiro you can easily join the central section of the Levada dos Tornos, Madeira's newest *levada*, and follow it to Monte – about a two-hour walk, if you don't stop at either of the two teahouses en route. Though not one of Madeira's prettiest *levadas*, it is the most accessible from Funchal and a good taster for other *levada* walks.

To reach the *levada*, turn right out of the Quinta do Palheiro Ferreiro and head uphill until you come to a junction (by two small cafés), where you turn left. Follow the road for 100m, after which the *levada* is clearly signposted on the left. At first, the *levada* passes close by the busy EN102 road above an unattractive block of council houses, but it soon plunges into shady, sweet-smelling eucalyptus woods, all the time running roughly parallel to the road, and crossing it at one stage.

After twenty minutes you are signed to *Jasmine Tea House* (see p.102), and there's another café, *Hortensia Gardens Tea House* (see p.102), ten minutes' further on.

The *levada* then follows the contours of the valley away from the road beneath more towering eucalyptus trees. Eventually you cross a steep road and pass a small weir just before a manor house, Quinta do Pomar. The path skirts the back of the *quinta* and rejoins the *levada*. Just past here you cross a road and within ten minutes you pass through the *Choupana Hills* resort. The *levada* continues through eucalyptus woods for another thirty minutes, when steps down to your left take you to the little village of Curral dos Romeiros. Head straight on through the village on the main track, where a wooden sign points you onto a cobbled track to Monte. The track winds down, round and up a steep, wooded valley before arriving by a church in Barbosas, a couple of minutes' walk from the top of the cable car in Monte.

continuing to run the estate today.

Buses drop you at the entrance to the gardens, from where a cobbled track leads down to the left past the back of the old *quinta* building to a coach and taxi rank. Just in front of the *quinta* you'll see the original chapel, with stained-glass windows in the turret casting coloured light over the bright walls. Beyond here, the public areas consist of a series of formal flowerbeds, topiary, ponds and lush lawns, which combine the formal English style with a tropical exuberance, epitomized by the mingling of blackbird song with the hum of cicadas.

▲ LEVADA DOS TORNOS

Less formal is the untended, overgrown ravine to the west of the gardens, known as the Inferno: a path leads down into a valley full of giant ferns and trailing morning glory vines before snaking back up to the entrance.

Balancal Palheiro Golf

☎291 790 125, ⊛www.palheirogolf .com. Horários do Funchal city bus #33 from Praça da Autonomia. Opened in 1994, the eighteen-hole Balancal Palheiro Golf was designed by Cabell Robinson and is one of the most spectacularly sited in Europe. It lies adjacent to the grounds of the exclusive hotel belonging to the estate, the Casa Velha do Palheiro. If you don't

mind paying through the nose, you can take tea or drinks in the hotel bar or on the lawns in front.

Hotels

Choupana Hills

Travessa do Largo da Choupana, Choupana ☎291 206 020, ⊛www .choupanahills.com. Set in rural isolation with a fantastic perspective over Funchal, this deluxe spa hotel has rooms in Eastern-influenced wooden bungalows. Each has a balcony while, inside, the low furniture contributes to a Zen-like calm. The pagoda-like main building contains a designer bar, restaurant (see below) and top-of-the-range spa facilities, as well as an indoor and outdoor pool. The latter overlooks the

Levada dos Tornos that passes right through the grounds. €272 (inland views) up to €313 for sea views.

Quinta do Monte

Caminho do Monte 192, Monte ☎291 780 100, ⊛www.charminghotels madeira.com. Most of the rooms at this lovely hotel above the Jardins Tropicais do Monte are in a modern extension of an old *quinta*, which retains its sumptuous grounds. Rooms are large and in contemporary style with balconies, cable TV and air conditioning – the best ones face the distant Atlantic. The original *quinta* now houses a bar and lounge, while other communal facilities include a pool, gym and Turkish bath. €155.

Cafés

Hortensia Gardens Tea House

Caminho dos Pretos 89, São João Latrão. Daily 9am–6pm. Signposted off the Levada dos Tornos and by the stop for bus #47 to Funchal, this place boasts lovely gardens, a couple of terraces and an attractive interior with superb vistas. It also offers a wide range of Portuguese food along with home-baked bread, tea and scones.

Jasmine Tea House

Caminho dos Pretos 40, São João Latrão. May–Sept 10am–6pm, Oct–April 10am–5pm. A well-known English-run teahouse which cashes in on its position on the *levada* walk. Reached by a series of steep steps, it seems to have been beamed in from some south of England coastal town, complete with corny wall signs, framed cartoons and a patio garden with ornamental fountain. Dishes include tea and scones, some good broth-like soups and an impressive range of fruit and herbal teas.

Café do Monte

Caminho dos Barbosas 8, Monte. Daily 10am–6pm. Right below the entrance to the cable car, this bustling modern café has a

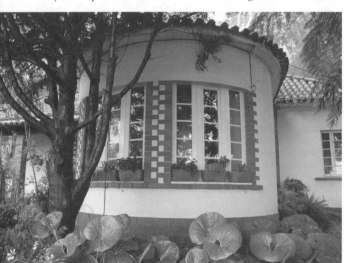

▲ HORTENSIA GARDENS TEA ROOMS

▲ HORTENSIA GARDENS TEA ROOMS

cobbled terrace with sweeping views. Inside you're spoilt for choice with various drinks, snacks and pastries. The set buffet lunch menu is usually good value, at around €10.

Café do Parque

Largo Da Fonte, Monte. Daily 9am–6pm. A café-cum-souvenir shop right on the main square, serving light meals (from around €7), hot and cold drinks, including a fine range of milk shakes. There's a roof terrace, though the best tables are those outside on the square itself.

Restaurants

Alto Monte

Travessa das Tilias, Monte ☎291 782 261. Daily 8am–9pm. Just above the main bus stop on Largo da Fonte, this is a fine spot for a drink or inexpensive light meal, such as good salads and superb homemade bread sandwiches. The interior is lined with old prints of Monte and the disused railway. Most people choose the outside terrace.

Belomonte

Caminho do Monte 184, Monte ☎291 741 444. Mon–Sat 8am–8pm. Just above the start of the toboggan run, the top-floor restaurant

here is one of the best bets for a cooked meal in Monte, offering reasonably priced Portuguese dishes and salads from around €6. The first-floor café is a popular, if smoky, retreat for the toboggan operators.

Quinta Terreiro da Luta

Terreiro da Luta ☎291 782 476, ⓦwww.quintaterreirodaluta.com. Daily 1–10pm. This doubles as a restaurant school, so, as you'd expect, gourmet Madeiran and international food is on offer – at a price, and reservations are advised. The setting, in the former station building of the abandoned Monte railway, is superb, with panoramic views, period decor and old prints of the railway dotting the walls.

Xoupana

Choupana Hills, Travessa do Largo da Choupana, Choupana ☎291 206 020. Daily 7–11pm. The *Choupana Hills* restaurant wins top marks for style and outlook, though you'll need to reserve a table and expect to pay €30 and upwards for a full meal. Soaring ceilings and designer furniture set the tone, while dishes such as superb mixed seafood and game whet the appetite. Unusual soups, speciality breads and sumptuous tropical fruit desserts top it all off.

Northwest of Funchal

Some of Madeira's most spectacular landscapes lie within a short distance of the capital. One of the most awe-inspiring is the sea cliffs at Cabo Girão, the world's second highest, and a dizzying sight from above. If you're feeling brave enough you can descend the cliff face in a glass-fronted lift to the neighbouring Fajã dos Padres. The cliffs can also be viewed from below at Câmara de Lobos, one of the few traditional fishing villages on the island; its claim to fame is that Winston Churchill often came to paint its pretty harbour. Inland, the remote village of Curral das Freiras, set in a valley surrounded by the island's highest peaks, gives a taste of the extraordinary mountainous interior of the island.

Câmara de Lobos

Câmara de Lobos, 8km west of Funchal, is one of the island's most atmospheric

fishing villages and is heavily promoted as the erstwhile favourite painting spot of

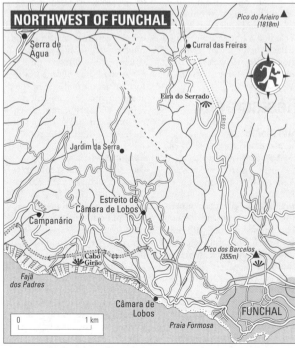

NORTHWEST OF FUNCHAL

Pico do Arieiro (1818m)

Serra de Água

Curral das Freiras

Eira do Serrado

Jardim da Serra

Estreito de Câmara de Lobos

Campanário

Pico dos Barcelos (355m)

Cabo Girão

Fajã dos Padres

Câmara de Lobos

FUNCHAL

Praia Formosa

0   1 km

▲ CÂMARA DE LOBOS

Winston Churchill (see box on p.107). Despite the rash of new development on the outskirts, the centre of the village, with its whitewashed houses, shops and bars, remains instantly likeable and charismatic. The stony beach doubles as the harbour, filled with colourful beached fishing boats.

The village was named after *lobos de mar* – monk seals ("sea wolves" in Portuguese) – which were frequent visitors to the harbour when it was first settled by Gonçalves Zarco in 1420, and have since become the symbol for Madeira. There are no monk seals here nowadays, however (they are one of the most endangered species in the world, forced to the remoter shores of the Ilhas Desertas), and the local fishermen who hastened their departure now make their living out of catching *espada*, scabbard fish. You can see the catch at the 7am **fish market** (Mon–Sat) in a concrete harbourside building, an atmospheric affair that is usually over within an hour or so, with market traders repairing to the nearest bar afterwards. Things are particularly lively on Sunday mornings, when off-duty fishermen fill the bars with animated conversation and play games of cards on upturned boxes in the harbour.

Câmara de Lobos: Nossa Senhora da Conceição and around

Rua Nossa Senhora da Conceição. The small but beautiful fishermen's chapel of Nossa Senhora da Conceição is said

Visiting Câmara de Lobos

If you have a car, the best approach to Câmara de Lobos is along the old coast road via the Hotel Zone (20min); take the highway and the journey time is only ten minutes. Câmara de Lobos is also served by Rodoeste bus #1 from Funchal (Mon–Fri 1–2 hourly, Sat & Sun hourly; 25min). Buses drop you off at **Largo da República**, a little square in the west end of town above a multistorey car park. The **tourist office** is just off the square on Rua Padre E.C. N. Pereira (Mon–Fri 9am–12.30pm & 2pm–5pm, Sat 9.30am–noon; ☏291 943 470) and can provide information about private *quartos* if you wish to stay the night.

to be the second oldest on the island, embellished with fifteenth-century pictures depicting scenes of shipwrecks and drownings in the life of St Nicholas, the patron saint of seafarers.

Câmara de Lobos: Igreja de São Sebastião

Rua São João de Deus. Located near the top of Rua São João de Deus, an atmospheric street full of traditional shops and bars, is the Igreja de São Sebastião, parts of which date back to the fifteenth century, though in the main it's an eighteenth-century confection, complete with Baroque altar, overbearing chandeliers and a sky-blue ceiling painted with clouds; there are also some attractive *azulejos*.

Câmara de Lobos: Largo da República and the promenade

Just to the west of the rocky bluff that splits the village into two, Largo da República offers fantastic views over the cliffs of the nearby Cabo Girão. It also

marks the start of the sea-facing Rua Nova da Praia, above a modern seafront promenade, both of which skirt round the bluff back to the harbour.

Câmara de Lobos: Henrique e Henrique

Estrada de Santa Clara ☎291 941 551. Mon–Fri 9am–1pm & 2.30–5.30pm. If you want to sample some of the local wine, head up Rua de Santa from Largo da República and you'll see huge barrels in the glass-fronted modern wine lodge, Henrique e Henrique. Dating from 1850, the lodge owns the largest vineyards on the island and produces some of the best Madeira wines around. There are free tastings and all the wines are for sale.

Estreito de Câmara de Lobos and the Levada do Norte

Rodoeste bus #3 (3–7 daily; 50min) and #137 (7–15 daily; 1hr). The road from Câmara de Lobos to Cabo Girão winds 10km up through traditionally terraced vineyards to **Estreito de Câmara de Lobos**, the centre of one of Madeira's most important wine-producing areas. The village comes alive during the September Madeira Wine Festival, when the harvest is celebrated with traditional bare-foot wine treading and folk dancing. At other times it is decidedly quiet, but a very attractive place to stop off, centred on a nineteenth-century church, with superb

▲ FISHERMEN PLAYING CARDS, CÂMARA DE LOBOS

views over the surrounding valleys. There's also a lively covered market (Mon–Sat), downhill from the central square, Sítio da Igreja.

The village lies close to the **Levada do Norte** – you'll see signs off the

▲ CHURCHILL'S FAVOURITE PAINTING SPOT

main road – which offers some lovely walking opportunities. The *levada* runs north to the Encumeada Pass (see p.148), but the easiest walk from here is south to Quinta Grande (2hr 30min) and Campanário (a further 1hr 30min). The *levada* passes through verdant vineyards, with beautiful views over the coast. If you don't feel like walking the return leg you can get one of a number of regular buses (#3, 4, 6, 7, 107 and 142) back to Estreito de Câmara de Lobos.

Cabo Girão

Rodoeste bus #154 stops near the cliffs (Mon–Fri 5 daily, Sat 1 daily; 1hr). The sea cliffs of Cabo Girão are the second highest in the world (after Norway), so named because Zarco got this far on his first exploration of Madeira's coast in 1418 before he did an about-turn (*girão*) back to Funchal. There is a small and, thankfully, well-railed *miradouro* right at the top, from which you can look straight down the 580m drop to the sea below, with fine views across towards the distant Hotel Zone to the

Winston Churchill in Madeira

A plaque in Câmara de Lobos harbour marks the spot where Winston Churchill liked to sit and paint during his stay on the island in 1950. Before becoming a politician, Churchill worked as a reporter for the *Morning Post* during the Boer War and visited Madeira in October 1899 en route to South Africa. Half a century later, following a heavy defeat in the 1945 general election and a minor stroke in 1949, he decided to return, hoping that the island would be "warm, paintable, bathable, comfortable, flowery" and the ideal place for him to write his memoirs. Churchill stayed at *Reid's* (see p.77), though the suite he was put up in was in a state of disrepair after the war years and ended up being partially furnished by donations from the island's British community. Here he wrote the fourth volume of his war memoirs, *The Hinge of Fate*.

When he wasn't writing, Churchill liked to paint. He travelled to Câmara de Lobos in a grey Rolls-Royce owned by the Leacocks, a wealthy family of wine merchants, who are said to have stuffed the Rolls' boot with drink to "help" him with his painting. Churchill's visit to Madeira was cut short when Clement Attlee declared a new election date, and he returned to Southampton by flying boat in late 1949 to campaign for what proved to be another defeat. He is still remembered fondly on the island, and *Reid's Palace Hotel*'s top room remains the Churchill Suite, much improved from the time he stayed there himself.

Wine production

Vines were one of the first plants brought over to Madeira by the early settlers (notably the Jesuits, who brought Sercial grapes from Germany, Vedelho from Italy, Bual from Burgundy and Malmsey from Crete), and the plants quickly thrived in the rich volcanic soil. The grape harvest on Madeira goes on for longer than anywhere else in Europe because of the differing altitudes at which the vines are grown. The lower slopes are harvested for sweet grapes from the end of August, then again in October or November, when Muscatel grapes ripen. The upper slopes produce the Sercial vines, which grow up to altitudes of around 700m and are the last grapes to ripen, producing a drier wine. Autumn sees trucks laden with fruit jamming the roads on their way to the wine producers.

Until recently grapes were trod in cement tanks called *lagars* – treaders were spurred on by traditional musical accompaniment – but today the majority are pressed mechanically. However, the foot-pressing techniques can still be seen during the September Wine Festival in Estreito de Câmara de Lobos and Quinta Furão in the north of the island (see p.176).

Most of Madeira's grapes are used to produce fortified wines (see box on p.74), although some of them go into locally produced table wines. These are young and fruity, a bit like Portuguese *vinho verde*, but little of it reaches the touristy restaurants: ask in local bars if you want to sample it. The only unfortified wines to be produced commercially are *Atlantis Rosé* – from the Tinta Negra grapes grown largely around Estreito de Câmara de Lobos – and *Atlantis Branco Seco*, produced from Verdelho grapes mostly in the north of the island. Both of these are drinkable, but not a patch on the wines from the Portuguese mainland.

east. It's a lovely and tranquil spot, at least when coach parties aren't visiting, with the smell of pine and eucalyptus in the air. Vines and vegetables are cultivated at the foot of the cliffs, though the fields are only accessible by boat. In the past, farmers reached some of the steeper slopes by lowering themselves down by rope.

Opposite the *miradouro* there's a small **café** (Mon–Fri 9am–4pm), with an adjacent exhibition space displaying art and photographs, usually related to the cliffs in some way. The cliffs are equally impressive from

▲ VINEYARDS AROUND ESTREITO DE CÂMARA DE LOBOS

the sea: there are half-day boat tours to the waters below Cabo Girão from Funchal harbour.

Fajã dos Padres

West of Cabo Girão is Fajã dos Padres, a tropical fruit farm with its own beachside restaurant in a spectacular location below 300-metre-high cliffs. You can park at the top of the cliff, from where an improbable and somewhat scary **lift** with glass doors (Mon & Wed–Sun 11am–6pm; €7.50 return per person) rattles down the sheer cliff face. At the foot, a path zig-zags down to a pricey **café-restaurant**, just above a stony beach where the calm waters are great for swimming.

The farm was once part of the vast Quinta Grande estate, originally owned by Zarco's descendants, but gradually sold to the Jesuits, who had acquired the whole estate by 1595. As well as farming the land, the Jesuits used Fajã dos Padres as a retreat, setting up a chapel, which has now been converted into an *adega* (wine lodge). The Jesuits ran the estate until their expulsion in 1759 by the Marquês de Pombal, who was suspicious of the power they wielded, and Fajã dos Padres passed into private hands.

The estate's sheltered position makes it ideal for growing vines, and the warmth radiating from the cliffs is also conducive to the growth of tropical fruits, such as mangoes, bananas, papaya, avocado, passion fruit and guavas. You'll need your own transport to get here, or you could join one of the frequent boat trips arranged though travel agents in Funchal for around €70 per person, including lunch at the café-restaurant.

Pico dos Barcelos

Horários do Funchal city buses #9, or #12 from Avenida do Mar, or #4 from Estrada Monumental (every 20–30min; 20–30 min). High above the Hotel Zone the tree-topped *miradouro* of Pico dos Barcelos enjoys sweeping views over the coast to the south and the impressive twin-spired church of Santo António to the north. If you want to pause longer, there's a handy café-restaurant here, too, the *Barcelos à Noite*.

Eira do Serrado

No public transport. Many visitors approach Curral das Freiras (see p.110) via the new tunnel, but taking the old road instead gives you a chance to take in Eira do Serrado, the site of a breathtaking *miradouro*. You can leave your car at the car park, and at the far side of a small tourist complex, a five-minute climb up steps takes you to

▲ CABO GIRÃO

a spectacular and hair-raising rock ledge, overlooking Curral das Freiras in the horseshoe-shaped valley of the Ribeira dos Socorridos far below. The valley, whose three sheer sides cut into the serrated peaks of Madeira's highest mountains, was mistakenly believed for many years to have been a volcanic crater, but it is now known that its dramatic geographical shape was created in large part by the river itself.

Back at the car park, behind the hotel, café and souvenir shop, you will see another cobbled track, which winds steeply down towards Curral das Freiras, a manageable sixty-minute walk away. Though sometimes closed because of landslides, it offers a very beautiful approach to the village – indeed, until 1959, it was the only way to get there.

Curral das Freiras

São Gonçalo bus #81 (Mon–Fri 13 daily, Sat & Sun 8 daily; 1hr 15min). Curral das Freiras is one of the most spectacularly situated rural settlements on the island, in a huge natural amphitheatre surrounded by some of Madeira's highest peaks. The village was founded in the sixteenth century by the nuns of Funchal's Convento de Santa Clara, who had fled the capital after a vicious pirate attack in 1566, when around a thousand French pirates looted the island over a period of sixteen days. The nuns sought refuge in a remote valley almost at the centre of the island, which they had traditionally used for farming, and the village that subsequently grew up here became known as the Curral das Freiras, "the Nun's Valley".

Neither the nuns (nor their convent) are around any longer, and today's villagers survive on agriculture and, increasingly, on tourism. Life revolves round the cafés and bars on the small **central square**, a superb spot, surrounded by a pretty collection of white, shuttered houses overhung with blossom, vines and orange trees.

Next to the square, steps lead down to the attractive town church, **Nossa Senhora do Livramento**, built in the nineteenth century to replace the crumbling older church, which had been built by the nuns. It contains some lovely *azulejos*, a painted ceiling, and – unusually for Portugal – attractive stained-glass windows.

Head up the side of the *Nun's Valley Restaurante* for lovely views of orange groves and flower-draped houses with little statues of birds and faces on the corners of the roof tiles.

One of the best times to visit is in November, when the village holds the *Festa da Castanha*, a lively chestnut fair.

▲ FAJÃ DOS PADRES

Hotels

Estalagem Quinta do Estreito

Rua José Joaquim da Costa, Estreito de

▲ PICO DOS BARCELOS VIEWPOINT

Câmara de Lobos ☎291 910 530, ✉www.charminghotelsmadeira.com. A tastefully converted five-star *quinta* set in its own sumptuous grounds. Most of the deluxe rooms are in the modern extensions and come with cable TV, all mod cons, verandas and great views over the valleys around. There are also two restaurants, an outdoor pool, sun terrace and sauna, not to mention a lavender field outside for the ultimate feel-good smell. €200.

Restaurants

A Capoeira

Sítio da Igreja, Estreito de Câmara de Lobos. Tues–Sun noon–3.30pm & 6–11pm. Right on the main square with an upstairs room offering unbeatable views across the precipitous valleys below. Vast slabs of meat and kebabs are grilled on metal skewers over a huge fire at the back, along with other Madeiran dishes, at very good prices.

Churchill

Rua João Gonçalves 39, Câmara de Lobos ☎291 941 451. Daily 11am–11pm. There has long been talk of turning this restaurant, located just above the spot where Churchill liked to paint, into a museum, but for now it serves decent, if expensive, Madeiran food, including flambés and seafood platters. Most people head to the terrace

for drinks overlooking the harbour; you can eat out here or in the cosy wood-lined interior.

Coral

Largo da República, Câmara de Lobos ☎291 942 469. Daily noon–3pm & 6–11pm. A modern café-restaurant on the east side of the main square, with a superb upstairs terrace affording views over the sea and Cabo Girão. It offers a range of tasty, moderately priced grilled meats and fish.

Nun's Valley Restaurante

Curral das Freiras. Daily 9am–7pm. This is the most touristy place in the village, but superbly positioned, with a terrace offering sweeping views down the valley. The mid-priced menu

▲ THE VIEW FROM EIRA DO SERRADO

includes local specialities such as chestnut soup, banana cake and chestnut cake. The bar is also lined with local liqueurs made from walnuts, passion fruit and chestnuts: you can sample them first before buying. If this place is full, there's a *Nun's Valley II* just down the hill serving similar fare.

As Vides

Rua da Achada, Estreito de Câmara de Lobos ☎291 945 322. Daily noon–4pm & 6.30–midnight. Just behind the main market building in an upstairs room, this place is famed for its grilled meats; it's also a good spot to sample the local wines. Mains start at around €8.

Bars

Amarr à Boia

Rua Nossa Senhora da Conceição 8–10, Câmara de Lobos. Daily 11am–1am. One of the town's liveliest and trendiest bars, with doors at the back opening up to reveal views over the harbour. There's good music and the usual range of local and international drinks.

Bar Central

Curral das Freiras. Daily 7am–10pm. With inexpensive drinks and a local clientele – old men play cards in a back room – this is a fine place to hole up in, with great views over the valley.

A Ginja

Rua da Achada 13, Estreito de Câmara de Lobos ☎291 946 008. Daily 7am–midnight. A traditional old *adega* with wood beams hung with plastic grapes and walls lined with barrels; head here to sample inexpensive local wines and cider.

Bar No.2 é p'ra Poncha

Largo Poço 1, Câmara de Lobos ☎291 942 554. Mon–Sat noon–midnight. This bar specializes in Madeira's famous *poncha*, usually made from *aguardente* (a local rum), honey and lemon juice, but here they prepare an impressive number of variations, including *poncha* made with passion fruit, orange and a particularly lethal one made with absinthe. There's an upstairs room and a downstairs bar, though most people spill out onto the street.

Spatyum

Rua da Carreira 6–8, Câmara de Lobos ☎966 481 801. Daily 1pm–4am. A lively night spot serving a range of shots, *caipirinha* and *poncha*, which loosens tonsils for regular karaoke sessions. There are also large plasma screens, Internet access, frequent live music and an outdoor terrace for when it all gets too much.

▼ CURRAL DAS FREIRAS

Southeastern Madeira

Linked by the south-coast highway, opened in 2000, southeastern Madeira is fairly developed, with two modern package resorts at Garajau and Caniço de Baixo and the more traditional little town of Santa Cruz, which is developing into a resort in its own right thanks to a fine beach, bustling market and its own lido complex. Machico, Madeira's second town, set round a pebble and sand beach, is one of the island's most enjoyable and historic places, full of lively cafés and restaurants. Up in the hills, away from the coastal highway, the quiet village of Camacha is famed for its wicker trade.

Garajau

Empresa de Automóveis do Caniço bus #155 (Mon–Sat 16–18 daily, Sun 12 daily; 20min); and bus #109 (Mon–Fri 6 daily, Sat & Sun 3–4 daily; 20min). Perched on a rocky headland, Garajau is little more than a strip of modern cafés, restaurants, shops and one giant hotel. The village gets its name from the *garajaus* – terns – that nest on the cliffs round here,

▲ STATUE OF CHRIST, GARAJAU

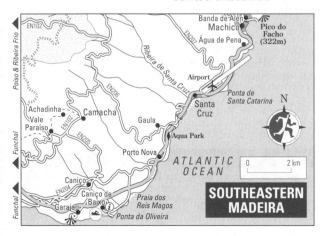

▲ DIVING OFF CANIÇO DE BAIXO

enclave, with German expats running several of the town's facilities.

The pristine waters off the coast are part of the Reserva Natural Parcial do Garajau, a marine reserve which extends from the high tide line to a depth of 50m. The best place to swim or snorkle is at the **Lido Galo Mar** (daily: June–Sept 9am–7pm; Oct–May 10am–6pm; Mon–Fri €3, Sat & Sun €4), reached via a lift, a short walk behind the tourist office. Here, a series of rock and cement sun terraces face a seawater pool and some slippery ladders that you can climb down into the clear blue sea.

You can hire out snorkelling equipment from the **Manta Diving Centre** (see p.199).

and it's the views from the cliffs that make the place worth a visit.

From the main strip a road forks to the right and winds down the cliff face past pristine new villas to a **statue of Christ** – a miniature version of those in Rio and Lisbon – more impressive for its location than for any artistic merit. Erected in 1927 on a rocky bluff, it offers fine views of Funchal and of passing tankers heading for the harbour. There are also picnic tables on the path to it, surrounded by spiky cacti and lizards.

Caniço de Baixo

The resort of Caniço de Baixo (Lower Caniço), 2km below the older town of Caniço, is made up of a string of modern villas and hotel complexes built on a low cliff. Its western end is its most appealing, a series of low-rise buildings set amongst lush vegetation and leafy gardens just back from the sea. You won't meet many Madeirans here: the resort is something of a German

Praia dos Reis Magos

East of the Lido Galo Mar, an attractive seafront promenade extends for around 1km past a cluster of modern hotels down the hill to Praia dos Reis Magos, a traditional fishing harbour, with a stony beach and jetty; you can swim here for free and, apart from the stones, conditions are just as good as at the lido. The beach has a much more local feel than the rest of Caniço de Baixo, though it can get crowded in summer.

Visiting Caniço de Baixo

Empresa de Automóveis do Caniço bus #155 serves the resort from Funchal roughly hourly, taking forty minutes. Buses stop near the **tourist office** (Mon–Fri 9.30am–12.30pm & 2–5.30pm; ☎291 932 919), just below the prominent *Hotel Ondamar*.

<p>

Caniço

Empresa de Automóveis do Caniço bus #2, #109 and #155 (Mon–Sat 18 daily, Sun 12 daily; 30min). Set on a hillside just 10km east of Funchal off the south-coast highway, the thriving satellite town of Caniço makes a pleasant stopover and is well stocked with restaurants (see below). It originally owed its wealth to its position on the divide between Madeira's two "captaincies", or governed districts, and it was for a long time an important agricultural centre. Today the town's most notable feature is its handsome Baroque church, which dominates one side of the attractive central square, Largo Padre Lomelino. Just south of here are sumptuous botanical gardens attached to the luxury *Quinta Splendida* and open to non-guests.

Camacha

São Gonçalo bus #29, every 30–60min; 30min. Set on a hill in the heart of the island's willow plantations some 14km northeast of Funchal, Camacha is the centre of Madeira's money-spinning wicker industry and is home to one of the island's largest handicrafts centres, O Relógio (see p.116) – an ideal place to hunt down souvenirs.

The centre of the village

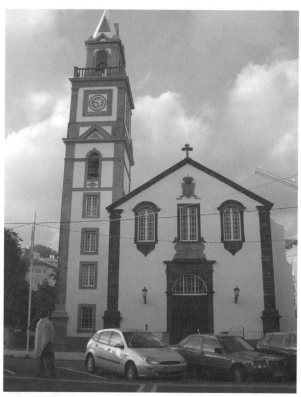

▲ CANIÇO'S BAROQUE CHURCH SQUARE

PLACES Southeastern Madeira

The wicker trade

Though wicker baskets had long been made in Madeira, the craft did not take off until the nineteenth century, when the same Hinton family that brought soccer to Madeira managed to persuade local farmers to diversify into wicker-weaving so as not to be over-reliant on the wine trade. There was soon a healthy demand for wicker – especially cane furniture – in Britain's former colonies. The industry has slumped somewhat since then, but better production techniques have helped craftsmen to make a wider range of products, and tourist demand keeps around two thousand workers employed in and around Camacha.

Wicker comes from willows, which thrive in the damp ground around Camacha. The larger branches of the trees are used like conventional wood, while the narrower, flexible branches are harvested in spring, then soaked, stripped of bark and dried to form wicker. Depending on the length of the branches, the wicker is then woven into baskets, furniture and other products.

is dominated by the Largo da Achada, a cobbled square the size of a football pitch – probably because it used to be one. It is said that Harry Hinton, a member of the wealthy Hinton family, who once owned the Ilhas Desertas, brought a football back from a trip to England, which led to Portugal's first ever game of soccer being played out on

▼ WICKER WEAVER, CAMACHA

Camacha's main square. To one side of the square, by a children's playground, a sign reads "Aqui se jougou futebal pela primeira vez em Portugal 1875" (Here football was played for the first time in Portugal, 1875).

A sign on the square points to the **Levada dos Tornos** (see p.100), which continues all the way to Quinta do Palheiro Ferreiro (around two hours' walk away) and beyond. To the north of the square, the Portela road heads uphill past the post office to the village's old church, a slightly run-down-looking Baroque building that seems to have been neglected in favour of the ungainly modern church below the main square, whose thunderous chimes ring out every quarter of an hour.

Camacha: O Relógio

The south side of Largo do Achada is dominated by the white O Relógio building, which has become the tourist nerve centre of the whole village. The building was once the home of a British merchant's family and was named after the *relógio* (clock) which was brought to Madeira from the parish church of Woolton near Liverpool by local doctor

Michael Grabham in 1896. Though the distinctive nineteenth-century clocktower still exists, the building has since been considerably altered, and today

▲ SANTA CRUZ

consists of a café, restaurant (see. p.125) and shop (see p.123). It also holds a regular slot for the island's most famous folk group, the Grupo Folclorico da Casa do Povo da Camacha, who play in the restaurant every Friday and Saturday night at 9.15pm (unless the group is away on tour).

Santa Cruz

SAM bus #20 (Mon–Fri 5–6 daily, Sat & Sun 2–3 daily; 50min). Despite its proximity to both the highway and the airport, Santa Cruz is a very appealing place – well worth a detour or even an overnight stay on your first or last night on Madeira. The town has a lovely palm-lined seafront and is centred on the attractive, white Igreja de Santa Cruz, one of the oldest and best preserved churches on Madeira, with its original sixteenth-century Manueline touches preserved intact. From the church, Rua Conégo César de Oliveira leads down to Praceta, a small square where elderly men hang out on benches under leafy trees and arbours.

Santa Cruz lido and seafront

The eastern part of Santa Cruz's seafront is taken up by a lido, Praia das Palmeiras (daily 9am–7pm; ☎291 524 248; free). There's a seawater pool and a separate kids' pool opposite the town jetty, and you can also hire sun umbrellas and loungers. Just east of the lido on a raised bluff are attractive public gardens, sprouting palms and dragon trees, with picnic tables offering fine views towards

▼ SANTA CRUZ MARKET

Ilhas Desertas. Next to the lido on Rua da Praia, you'll also find the small covered **market** (Mon & Sat 7am–4pm, Tues–Thurs 7am–5pm, Fri 7am–7pm, Sun 7am–1pm), one of the best on the island for fish, and selling every imaginable fruit and vegetable.

Extending west from the lido is the town **beach**, a long stretch of pebbles dotted with little palm shades and backed by palm trees, cafés and a big children's play area; when the sea's calm you can swim out to offshore bathing platforms.

Aqua Parque

Just west of Santa Cruz, signed off the main highway, lies a brand-new aquapark, complete with multicoloured slides, flumes and pools. Phone the tourist office in Funchal (see p.196) for opening times and prices.

Madeira airport

Though it may seem an odd tourist attraction, Madeira airport really is something special, as most visitors to the island find out. Opened in 1964, it was known as the "aircraft carrier" because of its incredibly short runway wedged on a hillside right by the Atlantic, and was considered one of the world's most dangerous places to land. Thankfully, an extension was opened in 2000 and now planes, including jumbos, can touch down on a spacious runway built on stilts over the sea – the coast road passes under the extension. Landing can still be a hairy experience, and in certain weather conditions planes are diverted to Porto Santo or, very occasionally, the Canaries. Madeirans are very proud of their airport, and you'll find postcards of various stages in its development all over the island.

Machico

Madeira's second town, Machico, lies just ten minutes' drive east of the airport in a beautiful natural bay, surrounded by steep, terraced slopes and fronted by its own stony beach. Though little more than an overgrown village, its laid-back atmosphere, restaurants and modicum of nightlife make it a great base for a holiday, or at least a night or two's stopover. One of the best times to visit is during the *Festa do Santíssimo Sacramento* (Festival of the Holy Sacrament) on the last Sunday

▲ MACHICO

Visiting Machico

There are various buses to Machico from Funchal; the best services are SAM bus #156 (5–10 daily; 1hr) or express bus #23 (Mon–Fri 4 daily; 55min). Buses stop at the main square, a short walk to the tourist office in the Forte do Amparo (Mon–Fri 9am–12.30pm & 2–5pm, Sat 9.30am–noon; ☎291 962 289).

of August, when a carnival-style procession culminates in a huge bonfire on Pico de Facho.

The focus of town is Largo Dr António Jardim d'Oliveira, the cobbled main square, where taxi drivers chat by their yellow cars in the shade of tall oak trees. The north of the square is taken up by the fifteenth-century **Igreja Matriz**, built under the orders of Tristão Vaz Teixeira's wife, Branco. Its most

distinctive feature is a gracefully arched Manueline door, with three small marble columns; the interior has an attractive painted ceiling and contains a statue of the Virgin.

East of the narrow Ribeira do Machico is an area of old fishermen's houses known as Banda de Alén, centred on the Largo Senhor dos Milagres, a quiet square where old men play cards beneath shady trees. On

PLACES Southeastern Madeira

ACCOMMODATION
Amparo   A
Dom Pedro Baia B

EATING & DRINKING
Azul Central da Cidra 1
Cantinho D'Avo   4
Mercado Velho   2
O Casco   3

MACHICO

0   100 m

Capela da Graça

Pingo Doce Supermarket

BANDA DE ALÉN

Police Station

Ribeira de Machico

Footpath

Igreja Matriz

Gardens

LARGO DR. ANT. JARDIM D'OLIVEIRA

LARGO SENHOR DOS MILAGRES

Pharmacy

PRACETA 25 DE ABRIL

Câmara Municipal

Capela dos Milagres

La Barca Discoteca

PRAÇA DO DR. JOSE ANTÓNIO D'ALAMADA

N

Forum

Mercado

Forte Nossa Senhora do Amparo

Praia

ESTRADA S. ROQUE

ACESSO MARITIMO

Capela de São Roque

Baía de Machico

Marina

Forte São João Baptista

the southern side of the square stands the simple, whitewashed **Capela dos Milagres** (Chapel of Miracles). Built in 1815, it replaced an earlier chapel said to have been constructed on the site where Anne d'Arfet (and possibly Robert Machin) was buried. This was destroyed by a flood in 1803, but miraculously a wooden crucifix survived (having been swept out to sea, it was rescued by a passing ship). The "miraculous" recovery of the crucifix is still celebrated every October 8 with a torchlit procession and a local public holiday on the following day.

Machico's seafront

Machico's beach, backed by a seafront promenade, palm trees and cafés, is very much the focus of the town in summer. At low tide the sea withdraws to reveal a narrow sandy stretch, onto which everyone descends to avoid walking on the large, steeply banked pebbles behind. The water in the bay isn't the cleanest, though its brown colour is caused by the mud sea bed rather than anything more

unpleasant, and there are usually sunloungers and umbrellas for hire.

The west end of the beachside promenade ends below a chapel, the **Capela de São Roque**, built in 1739 as a token of gratitude to the eponymous saint for saving the town from the plague. Unfortunately, it's normally locked, but if you do manage to get in you'll see some beautiful eighteenth-century *azulejos* showing São Roque, who dedicated his life to helping plague victims.

East of the beach lies the **Forte do Amparo**, a low, pale-yellow fort built in 1706 to protect the town against pirate attack. Passing pirates were a permanent menace to the local population, and Machico's forts were built so that soldiers could hole up after the women and children had retreated inland. Nowadays the fort houses the tourist office (see box on p.119). Just east of the fort lies the town **market** (daily 9am–6pm), with some appealing cafés. East of here, over the pedestrianized bridge, the bay has a much more

A brief history of Machico

Legend has it that Machico's name derives from Robert Machin, an English merchant who eloped from Bristol with his wealthy lover Anne d'Arfet in 1346. Their boat was thrown off course and blown against the rocks off Machico, and, although they managed to swim ashore with other members of the crew, Anne later became ill and died. Some versions of the legend say Machin also died here, others that the broken-hearted Machin buried Anne before he managed to escape from the island on a raft, before being captured by pirates and sold as a slave in Morocco. Here, Machin apparently related his woes to a Spanish slave, who, on returning to Iberia, spread Machin's tale. News of the Atlantic island eventually reached the Portuguese court, inspiring Zarco to search for Madeira. When he first landed on the island, Zarco was said to have found Anne's grave, leading him to name the place after Machin. A less romantic explanation is that Machico is named after Monchique, Zarco's home town in Portugal.

Either way, Machico was the first spot on the island to be colonized and was Madeira's capital from 1440 to 1496 under Tristão Vaz Teixeira, whose statue now stands in the main square. When the island was unified in 1497, the capital moved to Funchal, and Machico became a centre for sugar production and fishing.

▲ MACHICO'S BEACH

down-to-earth atmosphere, with fishermen hanging out their lines along the side of the road. The lines are phenomenally long (take care not to trip on them), as they are used to catch *espada* (scabbard fish), which live in deep waters only. The road ends at the **Forte de São João Baptista**, another town defence, erected in 1708 and later turned into a cholera hospital. Just below the fort, a jetty marks the spot at which the first ever Portuguese set foot on Madeira: a sign reads "Tristão Vaz Teixeira and João Goncalves Zarco disembarked here on 2 July, 1419".

Pico do Facho

The eastern side of Machico's bay is dominated by Pico do Facho, a 320-metre-high peak named after the beacon (*facho*) that used to be lit here to warn residents of approaching pirates during the early colonial days. The tradition of lighting a beacon is resurrected on the last Sunday of August, when a large bonfire is lit here to celebrate the *Festa do Santissimo Sacramento*.

With a car, you can reach the top by driving out of town for around 2km on the old road towards Caniçal and turning right 200m or so after *Restaurante Típico O Túnel* (if you pass through a tunnel you have gone too far) onto a side road signed Pico do Facho. Continue up the road until the tarmac runs out and becomes a dirt track; you can park here and walk the remaining 1km up the track to the peak.

Hotels

Alpino Atlantico

Rua Robert Baden Powell, Caniço de Baixo ☎291 930 930, ⓦwww .galoresort.com. Tucked away in a leafy side street, this is a relatively small hotel and better for it – 24 spacious double rooms, most with sea-facing balconies. There's also a small swimming pool. €92.

Residencial Amparo

Rua da Amargura, Machico ☎291 968 120, ⓕ291 966 050. A modern, friendly *residencial* built in traditional style, close to the seafront. Its twelve rooms are on the small side, but they are pristine and come with en-suite bathrooms and cable TV. €40.

Dom Pedro Baia

Estrada de São Roque, Machico ☎291 969 500, ⓦwww.dompedro. com. Machico's only high-rise building dominates the west side of the beach. The main block has reasonably sized rooms with good views over the bay, though no balconies – unlike those in the low-rise annexe next door. Four-star facilities include a pool in the small grounds, tennis, in-house restaurant and access to watersports facilities and diving (see p.199). €218.

Dom Pedro Garajau

Sítio Quinta Garajau, Garajau ☎291 930 800, ⓦwww.dompedro.com. A giant, rather anonymous and ageing three-star hotel, with some three hundred rooms divided into blocks, that takes up one entire side of the road into Garajau from Funchal. Rooms at the top of block one or two have the best views. There are studios with tiny kitchenettes for self-catering, though standard double rooms

are slightly larger. Facilities include a pool, table tennis and restaurant, along with access to a pool and tennis courts by the Cristo Rei. A nightly entertainment programme includes pianists, video nights and folk evenings. €80.

Inn & Art

Rua Robert Baden Powell 61–62, Caniço de Baixo ☎291 938 200, ⓦwww.inn-art.com. German-run restaurant and hotel offering a mixed bag of rooms, some of which are in a separate annexe up the hill with a small plunge pool. Best ones have great sea views. There are a range of tariffs and car rental options, with prices starting at €100 for a double room (with breakfast) or an apartment (without breakfast).

Quinta Splendida

Estrada da Ponta da Oliveira, Caniço ☎291 930 400, ⓦwww .hotelquintasplendida.com. If you are after a bit of pampering, this could be the place for you: an impressive hotel complex of rooms and apartments – each with kitchenette and balcony – set round beautifully landscaped

▲ GARAJAU PICNIC SPOT

botanical gardens, and most with views over the sea to boot (though you pay extra for this). There are two restaurants, two bars (one by the pool), a nightly entertainment programme, a fitness centre, Turkish bath and outdoor swimming pool. Double rooms from €112, double apartments from €120.

Residencial Santo António

Rua Cónego César de Oliveira, Santa Cruz ☎291 524 198, ℗291 524 264. An attractive guesthouse on the main drag to the beach from the church. *Azulejos*-lined corridors lead to large, clean rooms, each with their own bathroom, TV and either a balcony or terrace. Price does not include breakfast. €40.

Vila Ventura

Caminho Cais da Oliveira, Caniço de Baixo ☎291 934 611, ⓦwww .villa-ventura.com. A relatively small hotel by Caniço de Baixo standards, with 22 spacious studios, each with satellite TV, bath and balcony – though any sea views are partially blocked by the *Tropical Hotel* opposite. It also has a younger feel than most round here, with its own bar. It can rent out mountain bikes and arrange walks. Breakfast is €4.60 extra. €51.

Shops

O Relógio

Largo do Achada, Camacha. Daily 9.30am–8.30pm. A giant emporium best known for its wicker (see box on p.116). Just about anything that could be made out of wicker is sold here: baskets, chairs, seats, umbrella stands, shelving units, toys, plant holders, trays and hats. Bigger items are to be found on level-1, including a giant wicker boat and a menagerie of wicker animals, among them a ten-foot giraffe. If you should find such quirky objects irresistible, they can be delivered abroad. A workshop can be found on level -2, in which you can watch the stuff being woven. In addition, the shops sells just about any possible souvenir you could wish for from Madeira: ceramics, ranging from tasteful traditional Portuguese pottery from Alcobaça on the mainland to downright tack, place mats, *azulejos* tiles, liqueurs, Madeira wine and rugs.

Cafés

Cantinho D'Avo

Mercado Municipal, Machico. Daily 9am–9pm. A small café in the market buildings with an outdoor terrace facing the sea. Great snacks such as *pastéis de nata* and sandwiches, along with inexpensive dishes of the day from around €5.

O Canto

Praia dos Reis Magos. Daily 8am–8.30pm. A pretty café-bar in an old fisherman's house, with outside tables facing the beach. Good, light meals such as grilled sardines.

Esplanada Alameda

Rua da Praia, Santa Cruz. Daily 7am–1am. This attractive café with wrought-iron chairs and marble table tops sits on the seaside promenade beneath palms and facing the colourful beached fishing boats. It offers the usual range of drinks, snacks and pastries including great croissants and fresh juices.

Restaurants

Atlantis

Lido Galo Mar, Caniço de Baixo ☎291 930 930. Daily 11am–10pm. The lido restaurant is set on a terrace overlooking the sea and pool. Top service, fine buffet lunches and unusual evening meals such as *cataplana de espada com banana* (scabbard fish and banana stew) and *lombo de espadarte em casca de eucalipto* (swordfish roasted in eucalyptus bark). Around €10 for mains.

O Boleo

Sítio da Igreja, Camacha ☎291 922 128. Daily noon–3pm & 7–11pm. This place has a big outdoor barbecue and specializes in sizzling grilled meat dishes and *frango no churrasco* (barbecue-grilled chicken). There are tables inside and out and a list of daily specials such as stewed tongue. Full meals for around €12.

O Casco

Rua do Ribeirinho, Machico ☎291 962 150. Daily noon–11pm; bar open until 2am. With palm-frond sun-umbrellas and an outdoor patio,

▲ LARGO PADRE LOMELINO, CANIÇO

this is the best place in Machico for a good, no-nonsense, filling meal for under €12. Friendly service and a fine bar area, where you can hole up inside giant wine barrels.

Inn and Art

Rua Robert Baden Powell 6–62, Caniço de Baixo ☎291 938 200. Daily noon–3pm & 6–10.30pm. An arty restaurant, just west of the tourist office, with modern paintings on the walls, though most people head for the sea-facing terrace on a clifftop. The menu features light, mid-priced lunches and expensive full evening meals with dishes including fish, risotto and "chicken stew sweet and sour". There is usually a nightly live music programme, which ranges from fado to Brazilian.

Manjar do Atlântico

Estrada Garajau, Garajau ☎291 933 711. Daily noon–3pm & 7–11pm. Above the Sã supermarket opposite the *Dom Pedro* hotel, this place has an outdoor terrace, inexpensive set lunches for around €8 and a rewarding mid-priced evening menu featuring steaks, *picado* (Brazilian garlicky beef) and flambés.

Mercado Velho

Rua do Mercado, Machico ☎291 965 926. Daily 10am–10pm. The former small covered market building opposite the tourist office has been well converted into an attractive café-restaurant offering the usual Madeiran favourites, omelettes, salads and a few spaghetti dishes from around €9. The food is nothing special, but the setting – with seats outside on a cobbled terrace complete with a fountain and a few *azulejos* – is a cut above the rest.

Praia das Palmeiras

Praia das Palmeiras, Santa Cruz
☎291 524 248. Daily 9am–10pm, bar
open until 11pm. The lido café-
restaurant has a great sea-facing
terrace and good café snacks
such as *rissois de bacalhau*. Full
meals include a long list of meat,
fish, seafood, salads, omelettes,
pasta dishes and the speciality
steak. There is usually live music
on Friday and Saturday nights.
Mains from €8.

O Relógio

Largo da Achada, Camacha. ☎291
922 777. Daily noon–4pm & 7–11pm.
Despite the tourist trappings,
this is the best place to eat in
Camacha, mainly thanks to its
unbroken views over the south
coast and the Ilhas Desertas.
It can seem quiet when the
tour parties aren't filling up its
ample spaces, but the food and
service is top-notch. Moderately
priced dishes include omelettes,
spaghetti, steaks and a mean
range of desserts, including
chocolate mousse and ice cream
with chocolate sauce. When
not on tour, on Fridays and
Saturdays at 9.15pm, the Grupo
Folclorico da Casa do Povo da
Camacha, considered Madeira's
best folk music group, distract
your attention from the views.

La Terraça

Rua João Paulo III 30, Caniço ☎291
933 898. Daily noon–3pm & 6–11pm.
Head uphill past the church and
bag a seat on the terrace of this
restaurant, with great views over
the coast and the Ilhas Desertas.
The menu is quite meaty with
a few fish dishes, including
bacalhau, from around €9.

O Túnel

Estrada do Caniçal, near Machico
☎291 962 459. Daily 11am–10pm.

Located just before the tunnel
on the old road to Caniçal, a
couple of kilometres out of
Machico, this is a reasonably
priced place – as long as you
avoid the lobster or grilled
prawns – with fine grills and
outdoor tables offering great
views down over the Machico
valley. A handy stop-off on the
walk from Lorano (see p.133).

Vista Mar

Estrada Garajau, Garajau ☎291 934
110. Daily noon–3pm & 6–10pm.
Just out of Garajau on the
clifftop road to Caniço, this
place indeed has a sea view
(*vista mar*) from its tiny dining
room, which offers the usual
range of well prepared meat, fish
dishes, salads and omelettes from
around €7, and a fine *pudim de
maraculá* (passion fruit dessert).

Bars

Bar Azul Central da Cidra

Rua General António Teixeira de Aguiar
52, Machico. Mon–Sat 8am–8pm, Sun
9am–1pm & 3–8pm. A cavernous,
local, traditional bar, half given
over to selling handicrafts,
wickerwork, tacky ceramics and
other local souvenirs. Scores
high on atmosphere.

Clubs

La Barca Discoteca

Praceta 25 de Abril Machico ☎291 963
387, ⊕www.discoteca-labarca
.com. Fri–Sun 10pm–4am. The
town's only disco, so expect the
locals to be on familiar terms.
It would hardly set Ibiza alight,
but the music's pretty good and
the atmosphere friendly. The
€50 entry fee includes five free
drinks. Sunday is ladies' night.

Northeastern Madeira

The northeast of Madeira is a diverse, wild landscape offering some of the best walks on the island. To the east, you can hike the length of the precipitous and craggy headland of Ponta de São Lourenço, where you'll find Madeira's only naturally sandy beach at Prainha. The gateway to the headland, Caniçal was once the centre of a major whaling industry, now remembered in a fascinating whale museum. Inland, the island's top golf course at Santo da Serra is spectacularly sited, next to a village with a lovely park. North of here lies Porto da Cruz, one of the most picturesque villages on the dramatic north coast. From nearby Lorano you can walk the dizzying coastal path to Pico do Facho in the south.

▼ CANIÇAL FISHERMEN

Caniçal

SAM bus #113 (Mon–Fri 18 daily, Sat & Sun 10 daily; 90min). Although Caniçal is easily reached via a new highway from Machico, it's more fun to take the old road, bored through Pico do Facho in 1956. Before then the village could only be reached by boat or by hiking up over the peak. This remoteness made it the ideal site for the main processing plant of the odorous whaling industry, which set up here in 1949. Today Caniçal remains a pretty but earthy fishing village spread along a pebbly beach.

Just above the beach is the main square, where yellow taxis line up alongside the squat town church and the densely packed cemetery.

The jetty alongside the beach gets packed with kids in summer who share the space with brightly painted fishing boats. At the western end of the beach is the smart Complexo Balnear (bathing complex) with its own café-restaurant. Swimming in the sea pools costs just €1 for the day.

127

PLACES · Northeastern Madeira

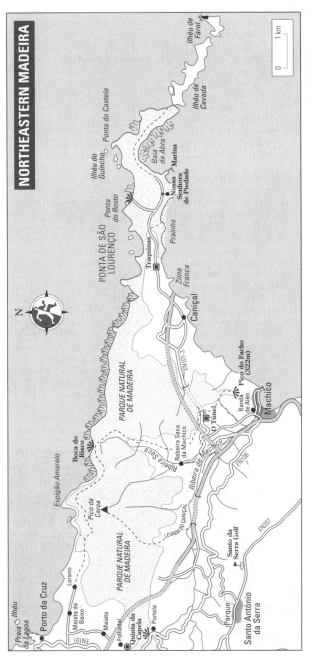

NORTHEASTERN MADEIRA

N

0   1 km

Praia · Ilhéu da Lagoa
Porto da Cruz
Lorano
Maiata de Baixo
Maiata
Folhadal
Quinta da Capela
Portela
Santo António da Serra
EN101

Parque
Santo da Serra Golf
EN207

PARQUE NATURAL DE MADEIRA
Espigão Amarelo
Boca do Risco
Pico da Caroa

LEVADA DO CANIÇAL
Ribeira Seca
Ribeira Seca da Machico
Ribeira de Machico
O Túnel
Banda de Além
Machico
Pico do Facho (322m)
EN108

PONTA DE SÃO LOURENÇO
Ponta do Rosto
Ilhéu do Guincho
Ponta do Castela
Traquinas
Zona Franca
Caniçal
EN101-3
Prainha
Nossa Senhora de Piedade
Marina
Baía de Abra
Ilhéu de Cevada
Ilhéu de Farol

The eastern end of the beach has been fenced off, marking the limits of the Zona Franca industrial complex. This incongruous collection of factories and modern warehouses was set up in an attempt to attract industry to locations away from Funchal, and has led to the construction of a new highway and Caniçal's increasingly opulent air.

Caniçal: Museu da Baleia

Tues–Sun 10am–noon & 1–6pm. €1.25. Caniçal is best known for its tiny Museu da Baleia, tracing the village's whaling industry. Whaling thrived in Caniçal until 1981, and the village was even used as one of the locations for John Huston's *Moby Dick* in 1956. To research the film, Huston and American star Gregory Peck joined the local fleet on a whale hunt, witnessing the death of some twenty animals, a fair proportion of the 250 whales – mostly sperm – that used to be killed annually off Madeiran waters. In 1981, an international moratorium ended whaling in these parts, and the coastal area off Caniçal became a marine reserve in 1986. The tiny museum squeezes in maps and examples of scrimshaw carved into boats, walking sticks and model mermaids. There is also a real whaling boat, roughly the length of the model thirteen-metre-long adolescent sperm whale alongside. The 16.5-metre-long lower-jaw bone of an adult sperm whale gives some idea of their size. There are also details of schemes to protect sperm, fin, humpback and blue whales that cruise past Madeiran waters today, along with other threatened marine species such as dolphins and the rare monk seal. Be warned that the gory video footage of whale processing and photos of kills may be upsetting to some children.

Prainha

A couple of kilometres east of Caniçal – and usually marked by a cluster of parked cars – steps lead down the cliff to the **beach** at Prainha, with, unusually for Madeira, wonderfully soft, dark-grey sand. The swimming off the beach is also superb, with crystalline water. Unfortunately, all this attracts a fair few day-trippers, especially at weekends

▲ WHALING BOAT, MUSEU DA BALEIRA

▲ PONTA DE SÃO LOURENÇO

in the summer, so space on the sands can be limited. However, you can always retreat to the terrace of the beachside café (summer only daily 10am–8pm; closed when the weather is bad), where you can get slightly pricey fish and seafood, snacks and drinks; the place also hires out sun beds and umbrellas.

Near the top of the steps that lead down to the beach is the chapel of **Nossa Senhora de Piedade**, which comes to life on the third Sunday of September, when a statue of Nossa Senhora de Piedade – attributed by some to an unnamed sixteenth-century Flemish master – is taken from the chapel to Caniçal accompanied by a procession of fishing boats; at other times, the chapel remains locked.

Ponta de São Lourenço

Madeira's craggy easternmost tip, Ponta de São Lourenço, has a very different feel to the rest of the island, at once exposed and barren, the spinning wind turbines at its southwestern end giving it a slightly eerie air. At Ponta do Rosto, there's a small *miradouro* with picnic tables facing dramatic cliffs. After

another kilometre, the road ends at a little car park – often occupied by a van selling snacks and cold drinks. Here people stop to admire the views over the sheer drops – some up to 180m high – round the **Baia de Abra**; you can also see the offshore islets of Ilhéu da Cevada and the lighthouse-topped Ilhéu de Farol. The geography of the landscape here is more like that of Porto Santo and the Ilhas Desertas than the rest of Madeira, and the vegetation is also distinctive, consisting of cacti, thistles and the red-tipped, seaweed-like ice plants.

Just above the car park there are picnic tables with superb views towards a rock arch at the far end of the headland, though there is little shade here and you'll find yourself in lizard territory – sit still enough and the reptiles will crawl up your leg and into your picnic.

The car park also marks the starting point of a **footpath** which takes you into the Parque Natural de Ponta de São Lourenço right to the tip of the headland, an exhilarating and, at times, vertiginous, three-hour return walk (see box p.130).

The Ponta de São Lourenço walk

The walk from the Baia de Abra car park to the tip of the headland and back (3hr round-trip) is one of the most dramatic on Madeira. The route follows a well-worn path, much of it over bare rock, clearly marked with stones, cairns, white posts or green arrows. Parts of the walk involve fairly steep scrambles over loose scree, and it can be extremely slippery when wet, so make sure you have good footwear. In winter, high winds can also make the walk hazardous, though the steepest parts of the walk have good fences for protection.

Start off heading east from the car park and you quickly pass a sign announcing entry into the Parque Natural. After five minutes, the path divides, with a faint downward fork leading to a lovely stony beach. The left-hand fork goes up to a viewpoint with great views over the north coast and huge cliffs falling into the sea. Continue on this path and after about half an hour from the start you cross bare rock, a fairly steep route. The path then goes over a narrow pass with views over the headland.

Around ten minutes later, you reach the steepest section, with wire fencing on one side leading you down to a very narrow neck of the headland with sheer drops, especially to the north side. The path then crosses fields lined with thistles and ice plants.

After about an hour into the walk, you'll reach the ranger's house, Casa da Sardinha. From here, you could detour southwest to the coast; a ten-minute walk brings you to a small jetty, Cais do Sardinha, where you can swim if the sea is not too rough.

Back at the ranger's house, the main path, somewhat faint at this point, climbs steeply to the east for another half hour to the very tip of Ponta de São Lourenço. The grassy incline suddenly ends in a dramatic cliff; the views from here are stunning. Allow another hour and a half to return the way you came.

Santo António da Serra and the golf course

SAM bus #20/78 (Mon–Fri 6 daily, Sat & Sun 1 daily; 1hr 45min); also São Gonçalo bus #77 (4–6 daily; 1hr). The small, unassuming hillside village of Santo António da Serra – or just Santo da Serra – is home to some of the island's best-kept villas, one of its finest parks and its most famous golf course, the dramatically sited

▲ THE PONTA DE SÃO LOURENÇO WALK

▲ TEE WITH A VIEW; SANTO DA SERRA

**Clube de Golf Santo da
Serra** (☎291 550 100, ⓦwww.
santodaserragolf.com), 1.5km
southeast of the village on the
EN207. Designed by Robert
Trent Jones, the 27-hole course
hosts the Madeira Open, usually
in February or March, attracting
international stars. At a height of
670m, the air is cool here, and
at times clouds float between
the golf course and the coast
below; if you are unlucky the
whole place will be swathed in
low cloud. Even if you're not a
fan of golf, it's worth sneaking
into the club house for a drink
to admire the stunning views,
encompassing the whole of the
eastern tip of the island and out
to the Ilhas Desertas.

Amid the green woodland
between the village and the
golf course lie flash *quintas* and
villas, belonging to wealthy
Madeirans and expats who have
built summer homes here from
the eighteenth century onwards.
The village itself does not have
an awful lot going for it. Buses
stop in front of the nineteenth-
century church; the church
once housed an important
Flemish work of art, nearly used

by the local priest as a wedge
to help a passing motorist who
had got stuck in mud here in
the 1930s. When, by chance, it
was discovered how precious the
"board" was, the rest of Madeira
was scoured for similar works of
art, leading to the collection in
Funchal's Museu de Arte Sacra
(see p.58).

In front of the church, the
main square is surrounded by
a few local shops and cafés
and a small children's play area;
just below here, you'll find
the Parque de Feiras, which at
weekends and holidays is given
over to stalls selling barbecued
chickens.

Parque do Santo da Serra

The extensive Parque do Santo
da Serra is great for families
and plant lovers. Wooden
gates mark the entrance, from
where a cobbled track, lined
with agapanthus, camellias and
hydrangeas, leads down into the
park woodlands. The grounds
were once part of an estate
owned by the Blandy family,
and you can still see the family's
pink *quinta,* now a government
office, as you enter the park on

your left. For children, there's
a nature trail to follow – in
Portuguese, but easy to translate
thanks to pictures of things
to look for. After a couple of
hundred metres you'll come to a
children's play area next to deer
and bird enclosures, along with
tennis courts and a crazy golf
course; at weekends, families
gather here for picnics. Beyond
this point, the path winds down
under pine and eucalyptus trees
to a *miradouro*, where you can
watch clouds scud up from the
valley above Machico and the
distant Ponta de São Lourenço.

Portela

SAM bus #53 (Mon–Fri 3–5 daily,
Sat & Sun 1–3 daily; 50min). A
new tunnel slices through the
mountains to the north coast,
but it's worth taking the slower
old road to Porta da Cruz via

the dramatic mountain pass of
Portela (622m), offering dazzling
views over the north coast, here
dominated by the giant cube-
shaped rock of Penha de Águia
(see p.172). The highest point
of the pass is marked by stalls
selling plants or souvenirs, along
with a taxi or two waiting for
walkers from Ribeira Frio (see
p.172). You'll also find a good
restaurant here, the *Miradouro da
Portela* (see p.135 for review).

Porto da Cruz

SAM bus #53 and #78 (Mon–Fri 5 daily,
Sat 3 daily, Sun 1 daily; 1hr 10min).
One of the most spectacularly
sited fishing villages on the
north coast, Porto da Cruz is
also one of the liveliest, as well
as being a good starting point
for the dramatic coastal path
that goes via Lorano across to
Machico.

Porto da Cruz's most
prominent building is a massive
modern church, a ghastly
structure with one external
wall lined with statues of saints
and a modernist tower stuck
at the front. But if you take
the steps below the church
to the **harbour**, you'll be
rewarded with stunning views
– on one side is the towering
rock of Penha de Águia and
on the other the steep cliffs
and terraced slopes of Pico da
Coroa.

The harbour is fronted by
a **beach** made up of giant
boulders and backed by
a small promenade. Most
people head to the west end
of the promenade, where
there's a superb large seawater
swimming pool, complete
with a special children's area
and café.

The promenade continues
west round a grassy knoll to
another stony beach, Praia da

▲ PORTELA PLANT STALL

▲ PORTA DA CRUZ SEAPOOL

Lagoa. It's a pleasant ten-minute stroll, past a little fishing harbour and over a sea cave, which spews spray and rumbles dramatically in high seas. Praia da Lagoa is backed by a big sea terrace, with changing rooms, a café and sunbathing areas. Alongside, with its distinctive brick chimney, is the Companhia dos Engenhos do Norte, a rum distillery – you can peer inside at the ancient machinery and giant wooden barrels, mostly containing the local *aguardente* firewater.

The coastal path from Lorano to Machico

Before the road over the mountains was built, the three-to four-hour **coastal path** from Lorano to Machico was the main route east. The path, which skirts the north coast's dramatic cliffs before a gentle descent to Machico, is at times precipitous and also passes through fairly dense areas of bramble, so be sure to wear trousers and walking boots.

From Porto da Cruz, it is a tough climb to **Lorano**, some 3km up the coast to the east, so it's probably best to take a taxi

straight to the village. Signed Maiata de Baixo off the main Machico road, Lorano is a small hamlet on either side of a dirt track. Continue along the track until it narrows into a path, after about twenty minutes' walk. A little further on the path splits; make sure you take the stonier upper path, which climbs steeply at first. Behind you are great views back towards Porto da Cruz.

After about an hour from the start, you round a headland and suddenly see Ponta da São Lourenço. For the next twenty minutes, the scenery changes dramatically, the dense undergrowth giving way to barren, exposed rock as you skirt the edge of a concave cliff. Watch your footing, especially when it is wet. Shortly after you leave the cliff, the scenery changes again as the path plunges through bracken, brambles and broom heather.

Around twenty minutes later, you emerge onto a grassy mountainside and soon reach the pass of **Boca do Risco** (the Risky Mouth) – so-called because when gales blow, the wind funnels through the pass, and crossing it can be risky indeed. Climb a small path to the right and you'll find a relatively flat grassy area, a good picnic spot.

Over the pass, the path descends into a wooded valley of pines (scarred by a fire in 2004) and, some half an hour from Boca do Risco, meets a tiny levada. Follow the levada to the left, and you'll look down on the village of Ribeira Seca do Machico, with its ramshackle, illegally built houses, and within twenty minutes you'll join the old Machico–Caniçal road.

Turn left and you can continue to Pico do Facho (20–30min). Alternatively, turn right and it's a minute's walk to *O Tunél* restaurant, from where you can call a taxi to Machico (around €6), or continue down the road (30min).

Hotels

Costa Linda
Rua Dr João Abel de Freitas, Porto da Cruz ☎291 560 080, ⊛www.costa -linda.net. Right on the seafront, and built in traditional stone, this modern hotel has a tasteful simplicity, with neutral decor and bright, fresh rooms, most with sea-facing balconies. €48.

Estalagem A Quinta
Casais Próximas, Santo António da Serra ☎291 550 030, ⊛www .estalagemaquinta.com. Just north of the centre of town on the Funchal–Portela road, this small, friendly place offers decent modern rooms with private bathrooms, TV and a small communal garden. There's also a games room, pool and a moderately priced, rustic-style restaurant (daily noon–11pm),

offering the usual range of meat and fish dishes, served inside or on a small covered terrace. €60.

Estalagem do Santo
Sítio dos Casais Próximos, Santo António da Serra ☎291 550 550, ⊕291 550 559. Four-star splendour just south of the park, ten minutes' walk from the golf course – golfers make up a fair share of the hotel's clients. Spacious rooms are done out in rustic decor and come with satellite TV; most open onto sumptuous lawns. There's also an indoor pool, tennis courts, jacuzzi and a restaurant. €100.

Quinta da Capela
Sítio do Folhado, off the Porto da Cruz–Portela road ☎291 562 491, ⊕291 235 397. This is serious get-away-from-it-all stuff, on a blowy hillside some 3.5km above Porto da Cruz. Set in a beautiful seventeenth-century manor house and chapel reached by steep steps up from the road, the building has national heritage status and is furnished with period pieces, including traditional kitchen implements. The *quinta* has five spacious and traditionally furnished rooms (though the bathrooms are modern) and its own gardens, full of agapanthus, from where you can watch buzzards swooping below you towards the coast. But, unless you have the legs of a donkey, a car is essential. €72.

Cafés

Beira Mar
Caniçal. Daily 8am–10pm. Right on the seafront, with outdoor tables facing the waves, this friendly café-bar serves drinks, sandwiches and tasty *doses*

(snacks) such as octopus, winkles and prawns.

Café Piscinas

Porto da Cruz. Daily 9am–midnight. This little glass-kiosk café has tables on decking facing the harbour, a great position to enjoy prawns, toasted sandwiches and the like.

Praia da Lagoa

Praia da Lagoa, Porto da Cruz. Daily 10am–10pm; restaurant 7pm–10pm. Smart, glass-fronted building facing the beach, with a range of sandwiches and snacks. In the evening, the inside area becomes a slightly pricey restaurant serving meat and grilled fish. The area out front hosts occasional summertime discos.

Restaurants

A Brisa do Mar

Complexo Balnear do Caniçal, Caniçal ☎291 960 726. Daily 10am–midnight. A swish, glass-fronted restaurant by the sea pools, serving superb meat, fish and very expensive seafood, such as prawns wrapped in bacon. Expect to pay upwards of €30 a head. For something simpler, there's also an adjoining café.

Miradouro da Portela

Sítio da Portela ☎291 966 169. Daily 9am–10pm. A bar-restaurant with two popular wood-panelled front rooms, warmed by log fires on cool evenings. If these are full, go to a spacious back room – without any views – with hooks in the ceiling from which

hang the house speciality: succulent meat kebabs skewered on long metal poles. The good-value menu also features salads.

Nossa Aldeia Restaurante

Parque de Feiras, Santo António da Serra. Tues–Sun noon–midnight. The best bet in town for unglamorous, but inexpensive, Madeiran fare, with a local feel. It is situated at the bottom end of town, just below the kids' play area: follow the sign to the right for "Parque de Feiras".

Pescador

Caniçal. Daily 7am–10pm. Just above the Museu da Baleia and the best place for a cheap and cheerful meal, with inexpensive meat and fish dishes and a few tables and chairs out front.

Praça da Engenho

Rua da Praia, Porto da Cruz ☎291 563 680. Daily 10am–10pm. Decently prepared, mid-priced Madeiran food is served in this cosy, stone-clad restaurant, set back from the seafront. There's also a café-bar area with better sea views.

Bars

Traquinhas

Estrada da Prainha, Rochinho (Caniçal) ☎291 960 556. Mon–Thurs 2pm–2am, Fri–Sun 2pm–4am. Marked by a flashing yellow light as you exit the new tunnel on the way to Prainha, this is a popular, laid-back bar with a friendly crowd where you can enjoy a drink or a game of billiards. Tables inside and out.

The west

Tourism has yet to make major inroads into the dramatic and unspoilt west coast, and only the lively town of Ribeira Brava has anything approaching resort status. Much of the rocky coastline is backed by steep wooded slopes, vineyards and banana plantations. The coast road links a series of small villages – pretty Ponta do Sol, historic Madalena do Mar and Calheta, a former sugar production centre with an artificial sandy beach. Further west, below towering cliffs, nestle Jardim do Mar, one of Madeira's most attractive villages and a burgeoning surf centre; and Paúl do Mar, another surfers' hangout. Above here, the wooded valleys around the village of Prazeres offer some superb walking country while, inland, Rabaçal is perhaps the most beautiful valley on the island and a base for more wonderful *levada* walks. Rabaçal marks the edge of the wild mountain plateau Paúl da Serra, a great destination for walking or a picnic.

Ribeira Brava

Rodoeste bus #7 (7–10 daily; 1hr 15min). Located at the foot of a dramatic gorge and endowed with an attractive seafront, the buzzing resort of Ribeira Brava makes a good day-trip from the capital. If you are here in June,

▲ IGREJA DE SÃO BENTO, RIBEIRA BRAVA

you should definitely stay over for the Festa de Saõ Pedro (June 28–29), celebrated with music, dancing and processions.

Ribeira Brava grew up in the fifteenth century as a staging post on the trade routes from the north to Funchal. Its sheltered position also favoured the cultivation of sugar, at that time the island's major crop. Ribeira Brava translates as the "angry river", a reference to the river which flows to the west of the town and still comes alive after heavy rains, especially in the autumn, though at other times it is a decidedly meek affair.

The main focus of the town is the pedestrianized **seafront**, giving onto a wide, stony beach and lined with a series of bustling cafés and restaurants; there are sunbathing areas and small sea pools to the west of the bridge. The town market,

137

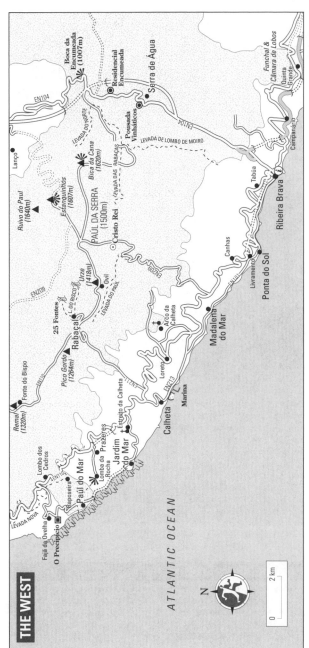

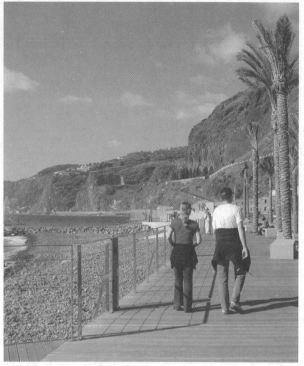

▲ RIBEIRA BRAVA SEAFRONT

decorated with attractive modern *azulejos*, and the main shopping street, **Rua Visconde da Ribeira**, are west of the tourist office.

The street also has some small, attractive public gardens, belonging to the Câmara Municipal (town hall), built in 1765 and originally the home of a local sugar merchant; you can still see bits of sugar-mill machinery dotted round the grounds.

Opposite the gardens on Rua dos Camachos stands the graceful **Igreja de São Bento** (daily 7am–1pm & 3–7pm), a sixteenth-century church with some wonderful Manueline touches, including a stone font and pulpit carved with plants and animals. The characteristic chequered-tiled roof is one of the most beautiful in Madeira.

Five minutes' walk north, at Rua de São Francisco 24,

Visting Ribeira Brava

Buses from Funchal pull in on the ER104 into town, close to the main church, while boats from Funchal moor at the jetty to the east of the bay. Located on the seafront is the **tourist office** (Mon–Fri 9am–12.30pm & 2–5pm, Sat 9.30am–noon; ☎291 951 675), housed in a small stone tower, the Forte de São Bento, originally built to protect the town from pirate attack.

is a small **Ethnographical Museum** (Tues–Sun 10am–12.30pm & 2–6pm; €2), set in a pink sixteenth-century town house, formerly a rum distillery and later a water-powered sugar-cane and cereal mill. Since 1996, it has been a museum dedicated to local crafts. Although the displays aren't exactly thrilling – fishing boats, mill equipment and looms – they do give an insight into the development of the fishing and weaving trades and the importance of wine and cereals to the area. There's a pleasant café here and some evocative old black-and-white photos of the village.

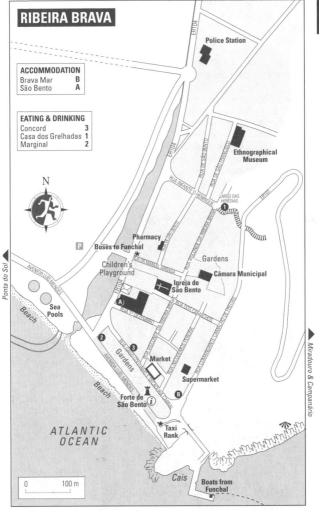

RIBEIRA BRAVA

ACCOMMODATION
Brava Mar   **B**
São Bento   **A**

EATING & DRINKING
Concord   **3**
Casa das Grelhadas   **1**
Marginal   **2**

N

Police Station

Ethnographical Museum

EFTL04

RUA DOS CAMPOS / RUA DE SÃO BENTO

RUA INFANTE D. HENRIQUE

LARGO DAS HEREDIAS

Pharmacy

Buses to Funchal

Children's Playground

Gardens

Câmara Municipal

Igreja de São Bento

RUA DO CABRITO

RUA DOS CAMACHOS

Ponta do Sol

AVENIDA LUIS MENDES

Sea Pools

Beach

Gardens

Market

Supermarket

Beach

Forte de São Bento

ATLANTIC OCEAN

Taxi Rank

Cais

Boats from Funchal

Miradouro & Campanário

0   100 m

Visiting Ponta do Sol

Rodoeste **buses** #4, #115 and #142 (1–2 daily) take around 1hr 50min to get to Ribeira Brava from Funchal. The little **tourist office** is just north of the church on Rua Príncipe D. Luís 10–12 (Mon–Fri 9am–12.30pm & 2–5pm, Sat 9.30am–noon; ☎291 972 850). Parking is scarce on the seafront, but there is usually space in the old tunnel, to the east of the seafront promenade.

Ponta do Sol

A quiet and pretty little village with a relaxed and lively air, Ponta do Sol is reputedly the sunniest spot on the island – its name means "sunny point". The population of just 4500 is shoe-horned into the folds of a steep valley, overhung with dense banana plantations; some 600,000 kilos of bananas are shipped from here to Portugal annually.

The town's Baroque church, **Nossa Senhora da Luz**, on Rua Dr João Augusto Teixeira, was built in the eighteenth century on the site of an older Medieval structure and contains some fine seventeenth-century decorative *azulejos*.

A plaque on a house at nearby Rua Príncipe Dom Luís I marks the birthplace of the grandparents of American novelist **John Roderigo dos Passos** (1896–1970), likened to James Joyce and known for his novels *42nd Parallel*, *USA* and *Manhattan Transfer*. The author, who visited the house, is now commemorated in the neighbouring Centro Cultural John de Passos, a modern cultural centre which often has exhibits related to him, along with other events.

The town **beach** isn't up to much, consisting of little more than a stretch of coarse grey stones. The palm-tree-lined seafront does have the perfect spot for a drink though – the balcony of the *Poente* (see p.151). Jutting out beyond the restaurant is the town's jetty, built in the nineteenth century, and the only link with the outside world until just after World War II.

▲ PONTA DO SOL

Madalena do Mar

Rodoeste bus #4 (Mon–Sat 2–4 daily; 2hr). Spread out along a stony beach backed by extensive banana plantations, the village of Madalena do Mar is said to have been founded by King Wladislaw II of Poland; after a disastrous defeat in battle against the Ottomans in Varna in 1414, Wladislaw disappeared and legend has it that he resurfaced in Madeira, having been offered asylum by King Dom João. He was granted vast estates by Zarco (see box on p.55), including the area around Madalena do Mar, and settled there after marrying a local woman. He concealed his identity and became known locally as Henrique Alemão (Henry the German – the locals mistook his accent). He died at sea when his boat sank off Cabo Girão and his body lies in the village church, the **Igreja da Santa Caterina**, parts of which date back to 1457. A painting that once hung in the church and now hangs in Funchal's Museu de Arte Sacra (see p.58) is thought to portray Wladislaw and his wife in the guise of Saint Arine and Saint Joaquim. The house where Wladislaw is said to have lived is just below the church – the one with a coat of arms by the door.

Calheta

Rodoeste bus #107 & #142 (1–3 daily; 2hr 30min). Calheta, a pretty village set in a steep valley just above the coast, has Madeira's only golden sand beach, though it's actually artificial. The seafront promenade links the new part of town that is

▲ NOSSA SENHORA DA LUZ, PONTA DO SOL

PLACES The west

growing up round the marina, just east of the beach, and the old town. Calheta was given its town charter in 1502 and was governed by Zarco's children. It later became a customs post for sugar exports, but waned in importance with the decline of the sugar trade in the nineteenth century. The attractive old town, with its neatly manicured gardens, sits on the eastern bank of a small river. Up the hill, the village church, **Igreja Matriz**, dates back to 1430, though most of it was rebuilt in 1639. Whilst its exterior is unexceptional, it is worth looking inside if you can (the church is often locked) to see a gloriously ornate and over-the-top ebony and silver tabernacle donated by Manuel I, and the Moorish-inspired Mudejar ceiling.

If you're interested in finding out how rum is made, visit the **Engenhos da Calheta** (Mon–Fri 8am–6pm, Sat & Sun 9am–6pm; free), a working

▲ CALHETA'S BEACH AND MARINA

rum distillery just below the church. You're allowed to wander round the rather antiquated-looking collection of cogs and wheels, used to grind, press and extract the juice from raw sugar cane. You'll also see the large fermentation vats, where the juice is distilled into *aguardente* white rum. There's usually a chance to taste the rums and *ponchas* or buy some from the souvenir shop.

Estreito da Calheta

Rodoeste bus #107 (1–2 daily) & #142 (1–3 daily; 2hr 30min). Though otherwise unexceptional, the hillside village of Estreito da Calheta is worth a detour for its sixteenth-century Capela dos Reis Magos (Chapel of the Three Kings), graced with some Manueline touches and a wonderfully vibrant sixteenth-century Flemish altar carving, of the Adoration of the Magi.

Jardim do Mar

Rodoeste bus #115 (Mon–Fri 1–3 daily, Sat & Sun 1 daily; 2hr 45min). Set below a steep, verdant hillside, the traditional fishing village of Jardim do Mar is an instantly likeable place, consisting of a warren of traffic-free, cobbled alleys, for much of the

Manueline architecture

Manueline architecture is a uniquely Portuguese style of architecture which emerged during the reign of Manuel I (1495–1521) and developed from the Gothic. The early sixteenth century was the age of Portugal's maritime discoveries and these provided the inspiration for Manueline motifs, drawn from ships' masts, ropes, anchors and the exotic animal and plant life encountered abroad and which frequently adorned windows, doors and columns. Many of Madeira's earliest buildings incorporated elements of Manueline architecture; some of the best examples are to be found in Funchal's Quinta das Cruzes (see p.62) and the Jardins Tropicais do Monte Palace in Monte (see p.96).

year laden with the scent of honeysuckle. You could easily while away a day or two here strolling along the beach or up into the banana plantations on the slopes above the village. It is also becoming a surfing centre, and hosts the annual leg of the World Surfing Championship in January, though this is the only time the place is remotely animated.

The centre of the village is well cared for, full of neat wooden street signs and carefully tended paths. From the main square, a road heads east to a little stony beach, which marks the eastern end of a seafront promenade that wends below the village. Follow this and you'll make out the village of Paúl do Mar to the west, set beneath its majestic cliffs (see p.144).

To the west of the village, above the church, a neat cobbled path leads past the local shop to a T-junction. You'll see a sign marking a footpath to Paúl do Mar, though the three- to four-kilometre walk is only possible at low tide. You'll need to arrange transport for your return journey, as the beach is not exposed long enough for a two-way walk. Check locally for tide information.

Next to the sign is a glass case containing a *rede*, a kind of hammock. These were

traditionally used as a sort of stretcher for ferrying around the sick or wealthy and would have been carried by two men known as *rodeiros*. In the nineteenth century, this particular *rede* was the favoured mode of transport for a local overweight priest who got his *rodeiros* to carry him as far as Ponto do Pargo, Calheta and even Funchal – the steepness of the cliffs round here make this seem cruel in the extreme.

▲ BANANA TREES, JARDIM DO MAR

▲ PRAZERES

Prazeres and the Levada Nova

Rodoeste bus #115 & #107 (1–2 daily; 2hr 45min). Prazeres is a small agricultural settlement clustered round a twin-spired church. It's a good place from which to start walking the nearby Levada Nova, which finishes at Ponta do Pargo (see p.152), taking in the village of Raposeira en route – a three- to four-hour walk in all. The Levada Nova is one of the island's most attractive *levadas*, winding through idyllic, largely wooded countryside. For much of the way it shadows the gentle gradients of the coast road 101. The *levada* stops above Ponta do Pargo, and a signed track points you down to the village itself.

A walk from Prazeres to Paúl do Mar

The *Hotel Jardim Atlântico* (see p.149) at Lomba da Rocha, near Prazeres, marks the starting point of a spectacular seventy-minute walk down the cliffs to the seaside village of Paúl do Mar. From the top of the cliff, the boats below look like tiny specks, and there is total silence but for the sound of cicadas and birds. Clearly signed steps to the far side of the hotel car park lead down the pot-holed cliff face – if you aren't up to the whole walk you could just descend a little way to a bench and admire the views from there (10min). From here the path descends dramatically; after a while you'll see a waterfall behind you, then you cross a stone bridge for the final section. A left-hand turn will take you to the quay of Paúl do Mar (see below). To avoid climbing back up the cliff again it's best to arrange someone to collect you or to order a taxi either from Prazeres or from the restaurant *Largo-Mar* (see p.151) in Paúl do Mar; the ride will cost around €20.

Paúl do Mar and around

Rodoeste bus #115 (Mon–Fri 1–3 daily, Sat & Sun 1 daily; 3hr). The road west from Prazeres passes a series of attractive farming villages, among them **Lombo dos Cedros**, a bucolic, leafy hamlet, surrounded by neatly cultivated terraces worked on by elderly, black-clad women. A little further west, a small flower-covered junction points you to **Paúl do Mar**, an unexceptional little fishing village, but worth a detour for its spectacular position beneath towering cliffs. Until the access road was built in the 1960s the village could only be reached by sea, and though it can be accessed by a tunnel linking it with neighbouring Jardim do Mar, getting to Paúl do Mar from the Prazeres road is all part of the fun, each loop and turn revealing heady views of the village below.

After the exciting approach, Paúl do Mar itself, however, is something of an anticlimax. There are some interesting backstreets round the church at its easern end, while the beach, obscured by a hefty sea wall, occasionally hosts surf competitions.

Rabaçal

Rodoeste bus #139 (1 daily; 2hr 30min). Among forested mountains high above the coast, Rabaçal is one of the most beautiful valleys on the island and the location of two popular *levada* walks: one to Risco Waterfall (3km), the other to 25 Fontes (3.7km). Just above Rabaçal, a very different walk can be had across rugged moorland to the Cristo Rei, a mini statue of Christ (see p.147).

To reach Rabaçal, you have to walk a single-track road for twenty minutes from a car park by a gravel *miradouro* viewpoint. Set in a breathtaking, densely wooded valley, its trees draped in lichens and mosses, Rabaçal is completely uninhabited and untouched by the outside world, except for a small government

PLACES The west

▲ CHURCH, PAÚL DO MAR

▲ VIEW FROM THE ROAD TO PAÚL DO MAR

the sheer sides at the valley's end, with the narrow Risco Waterfall spilling down a high mossy cliff. You can go quite close to the falls along the *levada* wall, but, as you approach, signs warn you not to proceed any further. The *levada* actually passes right under the waterfall, partly through a tunnel. Do not attempt to go beyond the sign, however, as the wet *levada* walls are precipitous and decidedly dangerous.

rest house, some public toilets and a few stone picnic tables.

A walk from Rabaçal to Risco Waterfall

Both *levada* walks start below the rest house and are signposted. The easier of the two is the one to **Risco Waterfall**. Follow the steps downhill onto the mossy Levada do Risco path. The path soon splits, the left-hand fork heading to 25 Fontes (see below). Keep to the upper, right-hand path which follows the *levada* through tranquil woodland. The valley becomes gradually steeper and narrower, and you'll see the distant, lower *levada* to 25 Fontes coming into view to the left. Around twenty minutes from the rest house you'll reach

A walk from Rabaçal to 25 Fontes

For a more strenuous walk – just over an hour one-way – follow signs from the government rest house to **25 Fontes** (going left where the path splits to Risco). Go down some steps and turn right onto the Levada das 25 Fontes; for a while it runs parallel to the *levada* to Risco, but at a lower level – indeed you'll see Risco Waterfall after about half an hour. At the head of the valley, at the point where you come to a small water house, you'll need to cross a river bed. The *levada* is quite

▲ RABAÇAL TO 25 FONTES PATH

narrow here, with fairly sheer drops to the left. After another thirty minutes you cross a path heading down to the left, but carry straight on for a further ten minutes. You then reach a sluice where a right-hand turn takes you to 25 Fontes – literally 25 springs, an enchanting jumble of little waterfalls and rivulets – though 25 is probably an exaggeration. This is a lovely spot to have a picnic, assuming there aren't too many other walkers who have got here first.

A walk from Rabaçal to Cristo Rei

From the car park above Rabaçal there is another interesting but very different five-kilometre *levada* walk, called the Levada do Paúl. It takes around eighty minutes and ends up at the **Cristo Rei**, a mini version of Rio's Christ statue, built in 1962 and also known as *Nosso Senhor do Montanha*, Our Lord of the Mountain. The walk starts at the small reservoir opposite the car park and heads off in a southeasterly direction – look for a tiny chapel marking the spot where the *levada* comes

out of a channel. You pass a couple of streams, but for the most part the landscape consists of lonely moorland, bracken and gorse, and you get superb views down to the south coast on a clear day. The *levada* crosses the EN209 – the road from Paúl da Serra to Ponta do Sol – a short way downhill from a car park just below the Cristo Rei statue.

You will have to walk back the way you came unless you want to chance hitching a lift on the little-frequented road.

Paúl da Serra

Rodoeste bus #139 (1 daily; 2hr 20min). Paúl da Serra, which translates roughly as "mountain plain", is a wild, high plateau. On clear days it can seem delightfully empty and fresh, with spectacular views down to the north and south coasts, great for walks or a picnic. When wind or mist sweeps across the boggy ground, however, it can be bleak in the extreme. The plateau is 1300m high and covers an expanse of moorland 17km by 6km, the flattest continuous area on the island. Little grows here except for

▲ ABOVE THE CLOUDS ON PAÚL DA SERRA

coarse grass, and the plateau is subject to low clouds and harsh winds. It's prime grazing land for cattle and is the only place on the island where it is safe for cows to wander freely without risk of falling down a precipice. Hardy shepherds can be seen tending their flocks, sheltering from the elements in the concrete huts that have replaced caves traditionally hacked into the boggy embankments. In summer, when bilberry trees bear fruit, local youngsters often come up to the plateau to camp. Bird-watchers are also attracted by linnets, goldfinches and the rare Berthelot's pipit, found only here and on the Canaries, while the sole buildings are the odd farm hut and the little hotel and café complex at Urze (see p.149).

▲ BOCA DA ENCUMEADA

Bica da Cana

Rodoeste bus #139 (1 daily; 2hr 10min). Bica da Cana is the impressive setting for another government rest house. The house is about ten minutes' walk from the main road up a stone track; there is a *miradouro* just above it at a height of 1620m, with fantastic views on clear days. The peak here is actually all that remains of a volcanic cone, from one of Madeira's most recent eruptions – some 890,000 years ago. In summer, this is a very popular picnic spot for Madeirans, especially at weekends.

From Bica da Cana the E204 begins to descend along the edge of a dramatic, craggy mountain valley and you suddenly remember how high up you are as the road pitches through rough road tunnels – keep your windscreen wipers at the ready as mini waterfalls often crash over the car as you enter or leave the tunnels.

Boca da Encumeada

Rodoeste bus #139 (1 daily; 2hr). A small lay-by at the junction of the EN204 and 104 marks the Boca da Encumeada, the "mouth of altitude", a mountain pass at 1007m, marking the highest point of the road linking the north and south coasts. On a clear day you can see the coast at São Vicente in the north and Ribeira Brava in the south; at other times you look down on a sea of white clouds.

Serra da Água

The mountain village of Serra da Água is a somewhat sprawling place without any clear centre. However, its position, in one of Madeira's most dramatic valleys surrounded by craggy peaks, is hard to beat and it's the site of the island's only *pousada* (see p.150).

Hotels

Brava Mar

Rua Comandante Camacho de Freitas, Ribeira Brava ☏291 952 220, ℻291 951 122. A modern seafront hotel at the eastern edge of Ribeira Brava. Three-star comforts include a pool and restaurant. Most rooms have a sea view. There are also suites and apartments for longer stays. €40, or €50 for sea views.

Calheta Beach

Calheta ☏291 820 300, ℗www .calheta-beach.com. On the edge of Calheta's sands, this modern four-star hotel block has its own pool, terraces, sauna, gym, satellite TV and restaurant; it can also arrange watersports and makes a good retreat if you just want an extremely quiet spot by the sea. €55, or €70 for sea views.

Estalagem Casa de Chá

Sítio da Estacada, Prazeres ☏291 823 070/1, ✉solprazeres@mail.telepac.pt. Located just before the church right in the centre of Prazeres, this modern low-rise place is tastefully decorated in traditional style with an attractive lawned garden at the back. All rooms come with satellite TV and a terrace. There's also a pricey restaurant and bar. €55.

Estalagem Pico da Urze

Ovil, Paúl da Serra ☏291 820 150, ℗www.picodaurze.com. On the remote Paúl da Serra plateau, this is a modern complex, consisting of a four-star hotel, shops and café-restaurant. All the rooms have balconies affording sweeping views over the moors,

and central heating – which you can need this high up. €40.

Estalagem da Porto do Sol

Quinta da Rochinha, Porto do Sol ☏291 970 200, ℗www.pontadosol .com. Perched on a cliff, five minutes' walk above Ponta do Sol, this sleek hotel was designed by local architect Tiago Oliveira. Rows of white cube-like rooms, with balconies and minimalist decor, sit on a steep terrace interspersed with lawns. The best rooms face the sea, others the town. There's a small indoor pool and a surreal clifftop outdoor one – its surface flush with its sun terrace – not to mention a clifftop bar for a sundowner or two. The glass-fronted restaurant does reasonably priced Madeiran dishes and pasta. €110, or €120 for sea views.

Jardim Atlântico

Lombo da Rocha, Prazeres ☏291 820 228, ℗www.jardimatlantico .com. For location this four-star development, five minutes' drive from Prazeres, is hard to beat. A series of apartments, bungalows and hotel rooms are stacked on the lip of a 400-metre-high clifftop affording dizzy views over the coast below. The main building contains studios (with their own balconies and kitchenettes), with apartments and bungalows (for two or three people) arranged on terraces below. The complex has its own restaurant, gym, pool, tennis courts, sauna, whirlpools, hydro-massage and a "nudist terrace" (popular with Germans). There's also a games room and live entertainment, even a hotel supermarket, while local walks and bike rental can also be arranged. €102, bungalows from €120.

Jardim do Mar

Jardim do Mar ☎291 823 616, ℱ291 823 617. Right on the main square, this plush hotel has decent-sized rooms offering exhilarating sea views, though the animal heads stuck to the corridor walls are off-putting. The hotel has its own bar and reasonable restaurant (daily noon–3.30pm & 7–11pm), with a superb sea-facing terrace. The hotel can also arrange windsurfing. €50.

Moradia Turística Cecilia

Jardim do Mar ☎291 822 642, ℮pontajardim@hotmail.com. Its balconies usually draped in drying wetsuits, this characterful guesthouse with its own sea-facing garden is a popular spot with local surfers, and offers simple, clean rooms. It's at the west end of town – follow the signs. €35.

Pousada Vinháticos

Serra de Água ☎291 952 344, ℮www .dorisol.pt. Madeira's only *pousada* (historic inn) is set in a stone building with a modern wooden annexe and a few separate log cabins. It has a friendly, Alpine feel with cosy, small rooms, leafy gardens and a highly rated restaurant. There is also a basement bar, a good place to hole up on cool evenings. Non-residents can use another bar just below the *pousada* (open daily 2–6pm). Best of all are the views of the dramatically rising peaks all around. €70, log cabins from €90.

Residencial Encumeada

Feiteirais, Serra de Água ☎291 951 282, ℮www.residencialencumeada .com. A couple of minutes south of the Boca da Encumeada pass, on the EN104, the *Residencial Encumeada* was built in 1999, but has a traditional feel, with tasteful wooden decor. Rooms are large and comfortable, each with a bath, TV and stunning mountain views from their balconies. The spacious downstairs bar-restaurant often fills with passing tour groups and offers reasonably priced grills and Madeiran staples. €40.

Residencial São Bento

Rua 1° Dezembro, Ribeira Brava ☎291 951 506, ℱ291 951 505. Giant, well-furnished, if slightly flouncy, rooms, some with sea views, in a modern, attractive building above a shopping centre. There's a sun terrace on the roof and a small downstairs bar. €40.

Cafés

Concord

Rua Gago Coutinho e Secadura Cabral, Ribeira Brava. Daily 6am–11pm. One of the best places on the seafront for ice creams, croissants and snacks served inside or on the attractive esplanade facing the sea, where there are tables under shady trees.

Joe's Bar

Jardim do Mar ☎291 822 242. Mon–Sat 8.30am–11pm. A lively café-bar selling fresh fruit juices at the western end of town by the local shop, with a little beer garden and a few benches outside on the street.

O Precipício

Fajã da Ovelha/Paúl do Mar ☎291 872 425. Daily 8am–10pm. A rather aptly named café-restaurant on the road from Prazeres down to Paúl do Mar. It really does feel as if it's on a precipice, especially when you're on the terrace. Specializes in grills, but also does a good range of drinks and snacks, with a mind-blowing view.

Restaurants

Casa dos Grelhadas

Largo dos Herédias, Riberia Brava. Tues–Sat 11am–3pm & 7–11pm, Sun 11am–3pm. Specializes in grills, as its names suggests, with dishes such as *frango no espeto* (chicken kebab) and *alheira da caça* (game sausage). Outdoor tables are set on an attractive raised terrace overlooking a little square. Very good value, with mains from €7.

Jungle Rain

Ovil, Paúl da Serra ☏291 820 150. Daily noon–9.30pm. Part of the *Estalagem Pico da Urze* complex (see p.149), this is a rather incongrous Disneyesque jungle-themed restaurant filled with mock flora and plastic jungle animals, complete with animal noises and a mini waterfall. If you're here with children it will seem like a godsend – there's even a special kids' menu – while for adults there are grills and pasta dishes from around €8.

Largo-Mar

Paúl do Mar ☏291 872 394. Daily 9am–9pm. At the western end of the beachfront, this is a good place for drinks or meals. Serves fine local fish, including *lapas* (limpets), *caramujos* (winkles), as well as grills at bargain prices; there are outdoor tables, too.

Marginal

Avenida Luís Mendes, Ribeira Brava ☏291 952 543. Tues–Sun noon–11pm. This first-floor seafront restaurant is a great place for beef, chicken or tuna, grilled over an open fire. Full meals for around €12.

Marisqueira do Camarão

Calheta ☏291 824 379. Daily noon–3pm & 7–11pm. Five minutes' walk beyond the *Hotel Calheta Beach* towards Madalena do Mar, this *marisqueira* serves decent lobster, seafood and mid-priced fresh fish, served on a sea-facing terrace.

Poente

Cais do Ponta do Sol, Ponta do Sol ☏291 973 579. Tues–Sun noon–11pm. Perched on top of a dramatic rocky outcrop overlooking the water, the *Poente* café is a great spot for a drink or a snack, especially at sunset. For a full meal, head to the restaurant over the road, partly built into the side of the cliff, but with good views from the upstairs windows and superbly cooked dishes including *lapas* (limpets) brought sizzling to your table. Full meals around €15.

Rocha Mar

Sítio da Vila Calheta ☏291 823 600. Tues–Sun noon–midnight. Opposite Calheta's marina, with a few outdoor tables and a moderately priced menu of tasty fresh fish and grills.

Tar Mar

Sítio do Piedade, Jardim do Mar ☏291 823 207. Tues–Sun 10am–11pm. On the cobbled lane to the beach, this restaurant offers snacks as well as fresh grilled fish and seafood inside or on a vine-covered terrace. Fine specials such as *arroz de lapas* (limpets and rice) for €16, other mains around €11.

Porto Moniz and northwestern Madeira

A trip to the northwest of the island is a must if you want to see Madeira's beauty at its rawest and most dramatic – even if the weather tends to be less clement. With its little lighthouse atop sheer cliffs, Ponta do Pargo marks the westernmost extreme of Madeira. In the far northwest, Porto Moniz's natural sea pools have attracted a plethora of hotels and restaurants, while nearby is the alluring walk along the Levada da Central. Heading east, the coast road hugs the dramatic contours of the mountains that spill down to the sea, connecting the picturesque village of Seixal with São Vicente, one of the prettiest on the island. Here you'll find a series of extraordinary underground caves and a volcano museum.

▲ THE LIGHTHOUSE AT PONTA DO PARGO

Ponta do Pargo

Rodoeste bus #142 (1–3 daily; 4hr). The small village of Ponta do Pargo, "Dolphin-fish point", was so named because Zarco caught dolphin fish (better known as sea bream) here while exploring the area. The village is surrounded by fields of vines and vegetables, worked on by hardy-looking women wrapped in headscarves and carrying huge bundles on their heads. At the village centre is an attractive church whose terrace overlooks

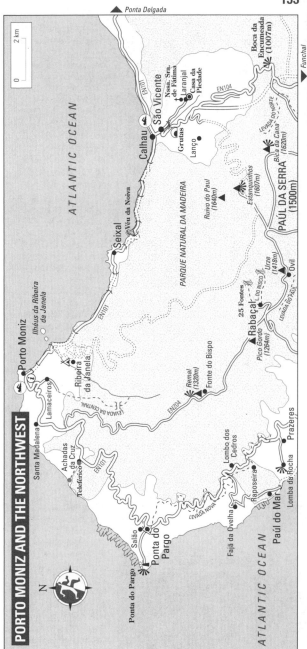

PORTO MONIZ AND THE NORTHWEST

0   2 km

ATLANTIC OCEAN

▲ Ponta Delgada

► Funchal

Porto Moniz
Ilhéus da Ribeira da Janela
Lamaceiros
Santa Madalena
Achadas da Cruz
Teleférico
Ribeira da Janela
Véu da Noiva
Seixal
Calhau
São Vicente
Nssa. Sra. de Fátima
Laranjal
Casa da Piedade
Grutas
Lanço
Boca da Encumeada (1007m)
EN101
EN104
LEVADA DO NORTE
Bica da Cana (1620m)
PAÚL DA SERRA (1500m)
Estanquinhos (1607m)
Ruivo do Paul (1640m)
PARQUE NATURAL DA MADEIRA
LEVADA DA CENTRAL
Remal (1320m)
Fonte do Bispo
EN204
25 Fontes
Rabaçal
Risco
Urze (1418m)
Pico Gordo (1264m)
LEVADA DO PAÚL
Ovil
Lombo dos Cedros
Raposeira
Prazeres
Lomba da Rocha
Paúl do Mar
LEVADA NOVA
Fajã da Ovelha
Salão
Ponta do Pargo
Ponta do Pargo
EN101

ATLANTIC OCEAN

N

▲ FONTANARIA, SÃO PEDRO, PONTA DO PARGO

road, turn right. If you're driving, follow signs for "Farol".

Spectacularly sited atop sheer cliffs that fall away into the sea, the **lighthouse** teeters, as it were, on the edge of Europe, and is the westernmost point on the island. The scrubby clifftop either side of the lighthouse makes a great spot for a picnic.

Just north of Ponta do Pargo you can join the Levada Nova, which runs east via Raposeira to Prazeres – see p.144 for details of the walk from the other direction.

fields and a lighthouse below. To the left of the church there is a recently restored fountain, the Fontanaria São Pedro, built in 1899 and covered with beautiful *azulejos* showing São Pedro (Saint Peter), Santo António (Saint Anthony) and cherubs. You can walk to the lighthouse from the church in about twenty minutes: follow the signpost to Salão de Baixo downhill past a farm and through low, twisted vines, and when the path joins a bigger

Achadas da Cruz Teleférico
Mon–Fri 8–9am & 11am–6pm, Sat & Sun 7.30–8am & 11am–6pm. €3 return. From Ponta do Pargo the EN101 cuts through remote countryside to the little village of Achadas da Cruz, worth a detour for its *teleférico* (cable car), built to help farmers tend their fields on a *fajã* – the flat, fertile soil at the bottom of a cliff, formed originally by landslides. The return ride affords superb views, though it's not for the vertigo-prone.

Porto Moniz
Despite being as far away from Funchal as it is possible to get, Porto Moniz is the north coast's liveliest and most developed town, with a cluster of cafés, restaurants and hotels gathered round its main attraction, two sets of natural **sea pools**, at either end of

▲ PICNIC SPOT, PONTA DO PARGO

Visiting Porto Moniz

Rodoeste **buses** #80 and #139 (Mon–Fri 2 daily, Sat 3 daily, Sun 1 daily; 3–3hr 30min) from Funchal pull up south of the harbour. Above the harbour you'll find the small but helpful **tourist office** (Mon–Fri 10am–3pm, Sat noon–3pm; ☏291 850 193). There is usually no shortage of places to park, unless you visit during the town's main festival, **Semana do Mar** (29 June–6 July), a week of sea-related festivities and events.

a seafront promenade.

The town was originally named Ponta do Tristão, after the nearby headland, which marked the dividing point between the two captaincies – the administrative areas run by Zarco and Tristão Vaz Teixeira during the early colonial days. From 1533, however, the running of the town was taken over by Francisco Moniz – who later married Zarco's granddaughter – and in 1577 it was renamed after him. Thanks to its sheltered harbour – protected from the elements by the offshore islet, Ilhéu Mole – Porto Moniz became a major

whaling centre when Azorean whalers set up here in 1939, but until tourism began to make an impact in the late twentieth century it remained a remote outpost, its residents relying on the produce of the steep terraces, which are still farmed in the traditional way. On the slopes around the old town you'll still see fields lined with drystone walls or fences made of heather broom, which shelter the vines and crops from the northerly winds.

Porto Moniz: new town

Porto Moniz's new town extends between the natural

EATING & DRINKING
Cachalote 1
Gaivota 5
Mar Vista 3
Polo Norte 2
Salgueiro 4

ACCOMMODATION
Atlântico A
Calhau B
Euro Moniz C

PORTO MONIZ

ATLANTIC OCEAN

N

Ilhéu Mole

Sea Pools

Aquarium

Sea Pools

SÍTIO DAS POÇAS

A

Centro De Ciência Viva

Taxi rank

Harbour

Police Station

Buses to Funchal

Pharmacy

THE OLD TOWN

Taxi rank

Câmara Municipal

ESTRADA REGIONAL EN 101

0   100 m

PLACES

Porto Moniz and northwest Madeira

The road from Porto Moniz to São Vicente

The sixteen kilometres of the old EN101 road from Porto Moniz to São Vicente is considered to be, in real terms, the most expensive stretch of road ever built. New tunnels now by-pass most of it, though you can still choose to drive on some sections when heading from east to west. The road was started in the early twentieth century and was completed by hand at a rate of about 1km a year – it took sixteen years in all. The road and tunnels had to be hacked out of sheer slopes and cliffs; at times workers had to be suspended by ropes to dig out the steeper sections. By the end of the twentieth century, the increased volume of traffic had turned the narrower sections of the thoroughfare into dangerous bottlenecks, so new tunnels have been cut along these sections, boosting the cost of the road, but making the route much less harrowing.

sea pools that have formed in the sculpted volcanic rocks. The easterly pools, below the *Restaurante Cachalote* (see p.162), consist of a series of interconnecting channels and shallow plunge pools, which get deliciously warm in summer, though sunbathing space on the surrounding rocks is usually at a premium. Further east, in an old sea fort, a brand-new **aquarium** is the town's latest attraction; the tourist office will be able to give opening times.

The pleasant seafront promenade, lined with kiosk cafés, continues west for 500m or so to the second set of more formal sea pools, most of which have been augmented with concrete. The €1 entry fee covers supervision and freshwater showers. Although the pools are shallower and less good for swimming than the set at the other end of town, there is usually more space to lay your towel down.

Porto Moniz: Centro de Ciência Viva

Tues–Sun 10am–7pm. Temporary exhibits around €5. Just back from the seafront promenade, the glass-fronted Centro de Ciência Viva (Centre for Live Science) hosts science-related temporary exhibits. Primarily aimed at locals, so not always with English labelling, the exhibits can be first-rate, some

▲ PORTO MONIZ SEA POOLS

having moved on from London's Science Museum. It also has a cybercafé and shop.

Porto Moniz: old town

While the seafront continues to sprout new hotels, the old town remains largely unaffected by tourism, its houses stacked up on the hill behind. The five-minute walk from the coast is very pleasant, especially during early evening when the air is cooler and the birds sing round the steep terraces. The village consists of low, white fishermen's houses gathered round a faded yellow church, with a terracotta-tiled roof and a neat clock tower. Just below it, you'll find a couple of banks with ATMs and a mini-market for groceries.

There are good views over the coast from here, but if you have your own transport, it is worth driving through the village and zigzagging up the hillside, where the outlook gets more and more dramatic. There are two *miradouros* at which you can pull in, the lower one with a handy café, the upper with a small shrine. Continue up this road for the start of one of the island's loveliest walks, along the Levada da Central (see below).

The Levada da Central da Ribeira da Janela

This walk (2hr 20min round-trip, or can be shortened to 1hr 20min) takes you up a dramatic valley into the UNESCO-protected lauraceous forest, some of the oldest surviving woodland in Europe.

To get to the start point, drive or take a taxi the 3km from Porto Moniz to Lamaceiros. Go through the village past the church, then head straight on down a track where the road

doubles back on itself. You'll see a small reservoir on your left: you can park here and walk down to the reservoir, to the right of which is the start of the *levada*.

The *levada* is easy to follow, with handy picnic tables set out at regular intervals and takes you past rows of agapanthus and hydrangeas, dazzling in summer. After five to ten minutes, on rounding a corner, you'll see the Ribeira da Janela river way below you in the valley on the left.

A few hundred metres further on, the path crosses a filtration plant. All along this stretch you'll see swifts swooping below you in the valley and hear scurrying lizards. After fifteen minutes from the start, you dive under the shade of dense trees until you emerge again to find a picnic table with stunning views

▲ PORTO MONIZ

▲ WATERFALL, NORTH COAST

down to the sea and the village of Ribeira da Janela across the valley.

After twenty-five minutes, you pass another picnic table, not long after which the *levada* briefly disappears under the path. Just beyond where it re-emerges you reach a sluice; walk along the side of the sluice – not up the path to the right – for more great views. The next section of 200m is lined with fruit trees, shortly beyond which is another picnic spot.

After forty minutes from the start, you'll see the top of the valley, a mass of dense green foliage – this is the lauraceous woodland. From here, the path narrows in sections, with gradually steeper drops. You can either turn back here, or continue for another thirty minutes, climbing the valley until the path ends where the *levada* disappears into a tunnel.

Seixal

Rodoeste bus #139 (Mon–Sat 2–4 daily, Sun 1 daily; 3hr). Seixal is divided into two distinct parts: the fairly dull upper town, with a few shops and cafés, and the far prettier lower town, a tranquil cluster of traditional houses, connected by steep cobbled steps and interspersed with vegetable plots and vineyards surrounded by heather broom. The backdrop to all of this is a spectacular coastline and towering mountains.

To get to the lower town from the main road, follow the signs for the *cais* (quay); as you head down the hill, look out for the Véu da Noiva (bride's veil) waterfalls pouring down the cliff and over a road tunnel further down the coast.

At the foot of the hill you reach a little harbour bobbing with fishing boats. You can take the steps down to the sea for some great swimming, or, when the waves get up, you can swim in the small sea pools.

São Vicente

Rodoeste bus #6 (2–3 daily); also bus #139 (1–4 daily); 2hr 30min. Sitting at the junction between the north-coast highway and the pass over to Funchal, São Vicente has always been a popular stopping-off point for Madeirans travelling from the north coast to the

▲ VIEW FROM SEIXAL

capital – and, more recently, its spruced-up **old town** has become similarly popular with tourists. The central zone is completely pedestrianized and ridiculously pretty, its narrow streets lined with flowers and neatly kept cafés and shops, all gathered round a lovely seventeenth-century Baroque **church** with a chequered spire. Inside, you'll see a painting of São Vicente – Lisbon's patron saint – on the ceiling and beautiful *azulejos* on the lower walls. In front of the church is a cobbled square, surrounded by palm trees and next to a carefully tended cemetery.

From the town you can also see the distinctive church tower of **Nossa Senhora de Fátima**, completed in 1953, on the hilltop opposite, splendid in its solitude against a backdrop of green mountains.

▲ SÃO VICENTE

Calhau

São Vicente's main car and coach park is in Calhau, 1km north, on the coast. Calhau consists of an appealing row of restaurants and shops facing a rocky beach. Though popular with surfers, the Atlantic here is usually far too dangerous to risk swimming, and copious amounts of driftwood get deposited on the stones – the wood is often burned in giant pyres on the beach. While at the seafront, take a look at the unusual **Capela São Roque**, by the bridge – a rock pile with a cross on it and a chapel embedded in its front, dating from 1692.

Heading east over the bridge, it is a couple of minutes' walk along the seafront to the Piscina Calamar (open daily; free), a lido in front of the *Estalagem Calamar*. There are **seawater pools** and ladders down to the sea – though you should avoid swimming when it's rough. The pools get very lively at weekends in summer, with most people adjourning afterwards to the adjoining café.

From the Capela São Roque there's a pleasant **shortcut** to São Vicente. Follow the old path just east of the bridge, which passes through a couple of rock arches and winds through undergrowth up the valley, until you come to an old bridge, which you cross to get to the centre of the old town – the walk takes about ten minutes, and bypasses the busier main road to the centre.

Grutas e Centro do Vulcanismo

Daily 10am–7pm; last entry 6pm; tours every 15–20min; 1hr. €8.

The Grutas de São Vicente is a dramatic series of underground caves, with the added attraction of an informative exhibition on volcanoes at the adjoining Centro do Vulcanismo. The entrance is marked by a car park on the right of the road, and the small café and exhibition space at the reception centre will help you to fill in time while you wait for the next tour.

The **caves** were blasted out by volcanic gases during Madeira's last eruption some 890,000 years ago; the longest cave is about 1km long and they descend to some 40m underground at their deepest point. Water slowly filters through the porous rock to form a series of clear, cold rock pools and streams – you may feel it dripping on your head. The caves have been lit and considerably modified since the Brit James Johnson stumbled upon them in 1855 – now you can walk upright comfortably, accompanied by gentle piped music. The tour, with multilingual commentary, guides you through most of the cave tunnels, their chocolate-coloured roofs rippled like mousse.

The tour ends at the Centro do Vulcanismo where you learn lots of facts and figures about volcanoes round the world, and an interesting video details Madeira's volcanic past. You can be transported in a shaking "lift" to the "centre of the earth", a rather tame hall of mirrors showing a replica earth's core, and don 3D glasses to view a very average film showing a volcanic eruption.

Hotels

Residencial Atlântico

Porto Moniz ☎291 852 500, ℗291 852 504. A friendly, modern *residencial*, located opposite the tourist office and done out in traditional style. Rooms are spruce and some face the sea; all come with private bathroom and satellite TV. €30.

Residencial Calhau

Sítio das Poças, Porto Moniz ☎291 853 104, ⊕www.residencialcalhau.web.pt. This imaginatively designed and friendly place has decent, bright rooms with private bathrooms and small balconies overlooking the sea pools. There's a sunny breakfast room and an upstairs games room with satellite TV and sweeping views. Good value and popular with students. €35, triple rooms from €45.

Casa da Piedade

Sítio do Laranjal (São Vicente) ☎291 846 042, ⊕www.madeira-rural.com. About 1km uphill beyond the São Vicente *grutas*, and set in its own lawned grounds, this idyllic white, terracotta-tiled eighteenth-century manor house makes for a great rural retreat. There are just six rooms, all filled with antiques, though they also boast modern comforts such as satellite TV and central heating in winter. Guests can use the kitchen and the communal lounge, with a log fire for cool evenings. €50.

Estalagem Brisa Mar

Seixal ☎291 854 476, ℗291 854 477. Decent, if simple,

▲ NOSSA SENHORA DE FÁTIMA

rooms with private bathrooms above a restaurant on the harbour front. There are great sea views from the front rooms, though not all have balconies. €30–50.

Estalagem do Mar

Juncos-Fajã da Areia, Calhau ☎291 840 010, ✉estalagem.mar@mail.telepac. pt. Just west of the bridge on the seafront, this fairly unattractive, but well-equipped, low-rise modern block has decently sized – and decently priced – rooms. All come with bath and TV and have either sea-facing balconies or open onto a lawned area near the hotel's outdoor pool, which is surrounded by neatly landscaped gardens. Other facilities include an indoor pool, sauna, gym, jacuzzi and tennis courts. There is also an in-house restaurant serving expensive traditional Madeiran dishes and seafood (daily 12.30–3pm & 7–9.30pm). €60.

Estalagem Praia Mar

Calhau ☎291 842 38, ☎291 842 749. This prominent, traditional-style, building with green shutters sits at the west end of the row of restaurants facing the sea. All the rooms are large and airy, though the front, upper ones – some with balconies – have the best outlook. €35, or €40 for sea views.

Euro Moniz

Porto Moniz ☎291 850 050, ⊕www .euromoniz.com. A modern high-rise with mostly sea-facing rooms, each with contemporary decor, balconies and cable TV. There is also a small indoor pool, a sauna and gym and a panoramic bar. Good value. €40, or €42 for sea views.

Campsites

Parque do Campismo

Ribeira da Janela ☎291 853 872. A new campsite set in rural solitude just east of Porto Moniz. Decent facilities and good nearby walks, but you'll need a car to get here.

Cafés

Estoril

Largo de Igreja, São Vicente ☎291 842 122. Daily 8am–8pm. Right opposite São Vicente's historic church, with outdoor tables on the pedestrianized square, this is the perfect spot to enjoy pastries, inexpensive snacks or drinks.

O Farol

Salão de Baixo, Ponta do Pargo ☎291 880 010. Daily 10am–10pm. This modern café-restaurant is built in traditional stone, a little uphill from the lighthouse. Along with sandwiches and soups, it does a range of well-prepared grills and salads from around €8. Also lets out good-sized rooms upstairs for €40.

Gaivota

Porto Moniz ☎291 850 030. Daily 8am–midnight. An all-purpose affair (bakers, *pastelaria*, café, pizzeria and restaurant), with a back terrace facing the sea and a good menu that features mid-priced pizzas, octopus and grilled chicken.

Restaurants

Brisa Mar

Seixal ☎291 854 476. Daily 8am–10pm. This smart establishment is the best place to eat in

PLACES Porto Moniz and northwest Madeira

Seixal, with a large dining area, snappy service and views over the harbour; the fresh fish is the thing to go for, though the salads and omelettes are equally good. There's also a downstairs club, *Kalhau* (see below).

Cachalote

Porto Moniz ☎291 853 180. Daily noon–4pm. Porto Moniz's highest-profile restaurant, open for lunch only, attractively built on the rocks right next to the eastern sea pools. There's even a mock tunnel inside connecting two of the dining rooms, one of which has space for 600 diners – it only gets remotely full when tour coaches pass by. The cuisine includes good-value fish *bouillabaisse*, lobster and the usual Madeiran dishes.

Ferro Velho

Rua da Fonte Velha, São Vicente ☎291 842 763. Daily 8am–2am. The menu of fish and meat dishes is somewhat limited, but this place wins thanks to its location in the heart of the historic centre and its shady outdoor patio. Inside, the pub-like decor includes international soccer scarves, from Ajax to Man Utd.

Frente Mar

Calhau ☎291 842 871. Daily noon–11pm. A welcoming, sea-facing café-restaurant, with reliably good Madeiran staples from around €8. Tables inside and out.

Mar Vista

Porto Moniz ☎291 852 949. Daily 11am–10pm. Friendly and popular with locals, offering a good range of fish, meats, salads and soups from around €9. It also has an attractive sea-facing terrace.

Polo Norte

Porto Moniz ☎291 853 322. Daily 9am–10pm. A smallish place offering good-value Madeiran fare. There's a bustling first-floor dining room, though best is the roof terrace, when it's open.

Salgueiro

Porto Moniz ☎291 852 139. Daily 10am–midnight. This is a good lunch spot, with a raised, sea-facing terrace, and serving fine soups, tasty garlic bread and a range of full meals from around €10.

O Virgilio

Calhau ☎291 842 467. Daily 10am–10pm. This place tends to attract more locals than the neighbouring restaurants on this stretch on the seafront. Inexpensive grilled meats and fish are served inside or on the veranda, and there's an attractive, *azulejos*-lined bar.

Bars and clubs

O Corvo

Rua da Fonte Velha, São Vicente. Daily 8am–1am. Any modicum of nightlife to be had in São Vicente can be found here, a small pub with an old still in one corner and bank notes pinned to one wall. There are low stools inside and a TV often showing live sport, with a couple of outdoor tables.

Kalhau

Cais do Seixal, Seixal ☎291 854 476. Daily 10am–4am. Bizarrely, one of the smallest villages on the north coast also boasts its best club. Hip decor and varied sounds, from sensual Latin to heavy dance. There's also a billiard table and chill-out zones.

Northern and central Madeira

Densely forested mountains rise up dramatically from Madeira's spectacular north coast. Much of the woodland is made up of lauraceous forest, so ancient it has been designated a UNESCO World Heritage site. On the coast lie the unspoilt villages of Ponta Delgada, Boaventura and Arco de São Jorge. Santana is famed for its triangular-shaped houses, and also boasts a fine theme park and a hair-raising cable-car ride. It is also the gateway to the island's best inland walking country, around Queimadas, and its highest peak at Pico Ruivo, which can also be reached on the superb peak-to-peak trek from Pico Arieiro. Equally impressive is the towering rock known as Penha de Águia, which casts a shadow over the pretty mountain village of Faial.

Ponta Delgada

Rodoeste bus #6 (2–3 daily; around 3hr). Overlooked by walls of forested mountains, Ponta Delgada is a quiet, traditional fishing village. The seafront is dominated by the Igreja do Bom Jesus, which becomes the focus of a religious festival in September, the Festa de Senhor Jesus, commemorating the survival of a wooden crucifix, washed ashore in 1470, presumably from a sinking ship. A chapel was built to house the crucifix, but this burnt down

▲ SEA POOL, PONTA DELGADA

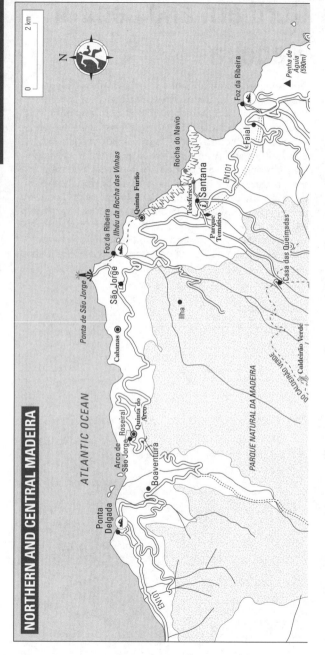

NORTHERN AND CENTRAL MADEIRA

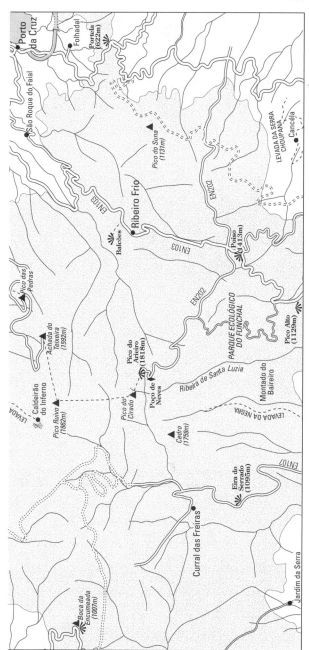

▲ BOAVENTURA

Boaventura

Rodoeste bus #6 (2–3 daily; 3hr 15min). Boaventura is a small, agricultural hillside village clustered round a church with a cobbled terrace. Just below the church, a sign points you to a *miradouro*, from where there are magnificent views of the coast and the verdant mountains to the north.

From Boaventura, the **old road to Arco de São Jorge** is one of the most dramatic in Madeira. It twists up the verdant, precipitous valley of the Ribeira do Pôrco before plunging through a tunnel and winding back down to the coast through more lush farmland and vineyards.

in 1908. The crucifix, however, survived the fire and, though charred, now takes pride of place in the current church, constructed in 1919.

A couple of hundred metres east of the church is the Piscina, a modern lido complex and the social hub of the village in summer. Here you'll find a deliciously fresh sea pool, changing rooms and a fine café-restaurant.

Arco de São Jorge Rosarium

Daily: May–Sept 10am–7pm; Oct–April 10am–6pm. €5. Arco de São Jorge is little more than a tiny village, but it does contain one of the most attractive self-catering villa complexes on the island, the *Quinta do Arco* (see p.176) and an impressive Roseiral (rosarium). With its entrance at the lovely old Quinta do Arco

The coastal walk from São Jorge to Quinta Furão

São Jorge's church marks the starting point of an exhilarating two-hour coastal walk to Quinta Furão (see opposite), via the pool at Foz da Ribeira. From the church, head towards the sea and take the first right at the small chapel. After around five minutes the road ends at a cemetery. Take the cobbled steps to the left and cross a narrow road; you'll pick up the path slightly to the right. From here it's a steep, winding, twenty-minute descent to the ruins of Calhau, an old port. Turn right onto the coastal path and after five minutes you come to the old bridge and lido at Foz de Ribeira, a great spot to cool off with a swim (see p.167). Continue over the bridge and you'll see the path in front of you, zigzagging up the hill. Just over an hour from the bridge, the path rejoins civilization near the neat lawns of the Quinta Furão (see p.176), where you can stop for a drink. From here it's a further 4km by road to Santana; you could get the Quinta to order a taxi or you could walk to the main road and catch bus #103 to Santana or back to São Jorge.

manor house, signed just off the main road, the rosarium is the largest collection of roses in Portugal. Come in summer when most of the thousand species are in bloom and the gardens are truly spectacular. Some of the rare and unusual species include climbing China roses, tea and damask roses and modern hybrids.

São Jorge

São Gonçalo bus #103 (2–4 daily; around 2hr 30min). The spruce little village of São Jorge (Saint George) is made up of well-kept houses set among vineyards and radiating out from an eighteenth-century Baroque church. The highly elaborate gold-leafed altar contains a statue of Saint George slaying the dragon and there are also some lovely *azulejos*. Behind the church, the *Casa de Palha* (literally "house of straw") is a traditional thatch-roofed building that has been maintained as a little souvenir shop and café, though the food is not up to much.

You can see other *casas de palha* on the pleasant fifteen-minute walk north of São Jorge to its little red-topped lighthouse on the Ponta de São Jorge.

A kilometre or so beyond São Jorge, a sign points left to **Foz da Ribeira**, consisting of sea pools by a small stony beach. It is a lovely drive to reach it, via a narrow road running parallel to the Ribeira de São Jorge past vineyards and neat terraces. The road ends by a stone footbridge over the river – the halfway point of the coastal walk from São Jorge to Quinta Furão (see box opposite). Here you'll find the Complexo Balnear de São Jorge, a modern sea pool, open year-round, with its own café-restaurant and superb views up the coast.

Quinta Furão

Dramatically sited on clifftops and surrounded by vineyards, the Quinta Furão is a hotel and restaurant complex (see p.176) run by the Madeiran Wine Company. During the September harvest (usually the second or third week of the month) tourists are encouraged to join in the traditional grape-treading – bare-footed, with men stripped to the waist. It's all totally geared to tourists,

▲ SÃO JORGE'S ALTAR

Visiting Santana

Santana's **tourist office** (Mon–Fri 9.30am–1pm & 2.30–5.30pm, Sat 9.30am–noon; ☎291 572 992) is just off the main through road next to the town hall. It is set inside a traditional Santana house – there are a couple of others that you can visit next door. Below the town church you'll find a supermarket, while opposite and just uphill there are a couple of banks, shops and local cafés.

but free and fun nevertheless. At other times, you can visit the highly rated restaurant. It also marks the start or finish of the walk to or from São Jorge via Foz da Ribeira (see box on p.166).

Santana

São Gonçalo bus #56 (1–4 daily) or #103 (2–4 daily); 1hr 40min. Santana, named after St Anne, is famed for its distinctive A-framed houses, one of Madeira's most familiar images (see box below). The village lies at the centre of some of Madeira's most fertile farming land – it supports vines along with various fruits, including figs, mulberries, plums and kiwi fruits. The village itself, extending along the main coast road, is fairly ordinary, clustered round some neatly tended squares and a pretty church, though its proximity to some of Madeira's most impressive

mountain scenery makes it a handy base for a night or two. If your visit coincides with the February *Festa dos Compadres* or July's folk festival (see p.201), you'll see the place at its liveliest.

Santana: the Rocha do Navio Teleférico

Wed 9–10am, noon–12.30pm & 5–6pm, Sat & Sun 9am–noon & 2–6pm. €3.50 return. Below Santana's church, a signed road leads about 1km downhill through farmland to the Rocha do Navio Teleférico, an extraordinary cable car which plummets terrifyingly down a sheer cliff to Rocha do Navio, a cultivated *fajã* on a rocky foreshore. The service, though popular with tourists, is geared towards the farmers working on the *fajã*, hence the odd operating times. As you descend, there are fine views of the coast

Santana houses

Known in Portuguese as *palheiros*, or haylofts, Santana houses are tiny thatched houses. Consisting of little more than a ground-floor room with a platform wedged into the roof eaves – very much like an "A" in cross-section – they are unique to Madeira. Their low, squat shape is ideally suited to withstand the wet and windy Atlantic weather that often lashes the north coast, the thatched roofs reaching down almost to the ground to protect the interior from the rain. The upper rooms form sleeping quarters, while the downstairs area is traditionally used for storage or as a living area. People cooked outside to avoid the risk of fires, and toilets were also well clear of the living area.

The houses first appeared in the early seventeenth century, but lost favour during the last century as modern building techniques – and Madeiran living standards – improved. A few Santana houses are still inhabited – mainly thanks to government incentives to attract tourists – but the majority of them (and there are hundreds scattered in the valleys around Santana) now house cattle, with corrugated iron roofs replacing the expensive thatch.

and of a gushing waterfall spilling down sheer rock walls. When the weather's calm you can swim off the stony beach at the bottom.

Santana: Parque Temático do Madeira

Daily: April–August 10am–7pm; Sept–March 10am–6pm. €16, children under 14 €13, under 5s free. Set in seven hectares of landscaped grounds on a steep slope, the "Madeira theme park" is pricey, but a fun half-day out if you have children. The main attractions consist of various low, concrete pavilions offering multimedia shows on aspects of Madeira and island life: its people, environment, future and so on. The shows are a bit hit or miss and you'll probably want to have good breaks between each one or the novelty soon palls. Luckily there's plenty of space for children to run around, with a boating lake, cafés and shops as further diversions. There's also a playground, a toy train, a re-created water mill, models of Madeiran houses and historical forms of transport. The most interesting part, for adults at least, is the *artesanato*, a craft village with little workshops where people demonstrate traditional crafts such as carving and weaving.

▲ A SANTANA HOUSE

Queimadas

Inland from Santana lies one of Madeira's most enchanting and least-spoilt forest areas (part of the UNESCO-protected lauraceous forest). *Queimadas* means "burning" – traditionally people brought combustible goods to burn here, safe in the knowledge that the cool, damp air would prevent fires from getting out of control.

▲ CASA DAS QUEIMADAS

To get there follow the sign to Queimadas off the main EN101 just before the Parque Temático. An incredibly steep road leads to the **Casa das Queimadas**, an idyllic-looking thatched government rest house, used by forestry workers and overhung with dazzling red-flowered camellia trees. The inside of the place is pretty basic, but you can use its toilets if needed. In front of the house there are wooden picnic tables under tall trees draped with Angle Hair moss and lichens, next to bubbling streams, where geese roost in mini Santana houses – a great spot for a picnic or an afternoon chilling out, as many locals do at weekends.

Many people also come up here to walk the **Levada do Caldeirão Verde**, one of the best *levada* walks on the island (see below). If you fancy a shorter walk (30min each way), look for the sign by the end of the road which directs you onto a gentle wooded path to **Pico das Pedras**, a picnic spot on the road linking Santana with Achada do Teixeira and Pico Ruivo.

The Levada do Caldeirão Verde

The three- to four-hour (13km) return walk along the Levada do Caldeirão Verde takes you through laurel woods and across some extremely steep terrain. Good footwear, waterproofs and a torch are essential and a jumper can be useful, as the air at this height is cool and most of the walk is in shade. Rainfall is also common.

The start of the *levada* is clearly signed from the Casa das Queimadas. Follow the path under ancient pine trees until you reach a gate, which you go through. Five minutes beyond here, a steep arrowed detour takes you down to the right round an unstable section of wall, but it quickly climbs to rejoin the main *levada* path.

The path narrows and you have to walk on the *levada* wall as it follows the twisting contours of the valley. After twenty minutes or so, you get superb views of the densely wooded mountains. Look behind and you can see right down to the north coast.

After about an hour from the start, the *levada* passes through

▲ PICO DO ARIEIRO, POÇO DE NEVES

four tunnels which get progressively longer and lower. In the third tunnel, keep to the side of the path to avoid deep puddles which collect against the tunnel walls.

▲ HOMEM EM PÉ

In the fourth tunnel watch your head, too, as the roof is low in sections.

For the last half an hour, you'll be walking on a *levada* wall that is just 40cm wide with fairly steep drops. At one stage you pass a huge stump of a lily-of-the-valley tree thought to be over eight hundred years old. Finally, after around ninety minutes into the walk, you'll reach a green amphitheatre of moss-covered rock, the **Caldeirão Verde**. A small path leads to the bottom of a waterfall trickling into a small lake, a pleasant spot for a picnic. The *levada* path continues, partly up steps, to Caldeirão do Inferno (Cauldron of Hell), an even more impressive waterfall about an hour further on, but it is a tough, tricky stretch, and unless you are an experienced walker it is best to turn back at Caldeirão Verde.

Pico Ruivo and around

At 1862m, Pico Ruivo (Redhead Peak) is Madeira's highest point, offering the most breathtaking views over the island. Despite its height, the peak is relatively accessible by car on the narrow EN101-5 road (clearly signposted off the main EN101 coast road) from Santana to Achada do Teixeira. Around 10km from Santana, the road passes **Pico das Pedras**, an attractive wooded picnic spot and a good base for some local walks. The road then climbs onto the barer lower slopes of Pico Ruivo until it ends some 15km beyond Pico das Pedras at a car park next to the somewhat ungainly **Achada do Teixeira** government rest house. Behind the house is an impressive series of natural basalt columns known as **Homem em Pé**, the "standing man". The grassy surrounds make a good place for a picnic and on a clear day you can see right down to the north coast from here.

Back at the car park, you will see the start of a paved path to the **summit** of Pico Ruivo, a relatively easy walk along a flat ridge; allow around an hour and a half to two hours return. After forty minutes you'll see Pico Ruivo's government rest house, a small white building. Just before here a path heads off steeply to the left; this leads on to Pico do Arieiro (see p.173).

From the government rest house, it's a steep but short climb to a viewing platform at the summit. It's a wonderful spot: wisps of cloud and smoke-like mist drift below you or creep up from the valleys, and

Northern and central Madeira **PLACES**

▲ CAFÉ FAIAL

there is complete silence apart from the sound of the wind and the odd hardy bird. To the southwest, the valley sides tumble down to the tiny red rooftops of Curral das Freiras (see p.110), while to the west spin the distant wind turbines on Pául da Serra, almost at the same height. Southeast lie the huge craggy peaks of Pico das Torres and Pico Ariero.

Penha de Águia, Faial and around

SAM bus #53 and #78 (1–5 daily; 1hr 25min). It is easy to see why Penha de Águia, a sheer-sided rocky cube, means Eagle Rock. It rises to 590m, its lower half terraced into fields, the upper half a craggy wilderness where ospreys nest. A small road skirts the lower slopes of the rock and there are extremely tough footpaths up to its summit – about an hour and a half's climb, and only suitable for the very fit.

Otherwise, the best place to contemplate its beauty is from the quiet hillside village of **Faial**, which takes its name from an evergreen shrub, the wax myrtle (*faia* in Portuguese)

that grows in the area. The best views are from its cobbled square centred on a substantial oak tree. The nearby church is the focal point of an annual *romaria*, a lively village festival held on September 8.

From Faial, a road bridge crosses the deep valley of the Ribeira Sêca. You can head under the new bridge to Foz da Ribeira do Faial, past a karting track to a little lido complex. A sea pool, kids' playground, rocky beach and a seasonal café attract a lively crowd in summer.

Ribeiro Frio

São Gonçalo bus #103 (1 daily; 1hr). Roughly halfway between the north and south coasts is the tiny village of Ribeiro Frio, "cold river" – named because of its high and secluded position in a wooded valley which gets little sun. But the cool air does not stop the flora from thriving: Pride of Madeira, hydrangeas and orchids give colour to the well-tended village gardens by the river. The village's main sight, however, is a government-run **trout farm**, set in attractive gardens with giant tree ferns and impressive topiary. Fed by several local *levadas*, the circular freshwater tanks are a teeming mass of swirling fish, from tiny spry to large trout, some of which end up on the menu of the local restaurants.

The woodland around Ribeiro Frio is part of the lauraceous forest native to Madeira and forms the backdrop to some great walks, the most popular being the gentle twenty- to thirty-minute return walk to **Balcões**. Signed off the bottom end of the village, just after *Bar Faisca*, it's an easy walk, past luxuriant gardens and along a flat woodland path. Balcões is a wooden viewing platform, which offers sweeping views over the island's highest peaks. A tougher walk from Ribeiro Frio is signposted off to the east to **Portela** (see p.132), a twelve-kilometre hike taking three to four hours.

Pico do Arieiro

Although only the third-highest point on Madeira at 1818m – so high that the mountain top is often well above the cloud line – Pico do Arieiro's accessibility makes it the most popular of the peaks and attracts a steady stream of visitors. Get there very early or late in the afternoon to avoid the biggest crowds.

As the road climbs up the increasingly barren slopes, a small sign to the left points out the **Poço de Neves** (snow well), an igloo-shaped hut built in 1800. Before electric refrigeration, ice was stored here before being carried down to local hospitals; the ice was also used to supply gin and tonics at *Reid's Palace Hotel*.

From the summit car park, the views can be astounding, with both coasts of the island sometimes visible, though, more often than not, at least one of the coasts will be submerged beneath fluffy clouds, itself an impressive sight. If you're unlucky, the summit will also be shrouded in cold mist.

The car park marks the start of one of the most rewarding **walks** on the island, across to Pico Ruivo (see below). Another option is to walk just the first section of the route to Pico Ruivo, as far as Ninho da Manta (the **Buzzard's Nest**), clearly signposted off the main path. This is a relatively easy fifty-minute round-trip walk to a dizzy *miradouro* with fantastic

views down to the south coast. Remember, however, that the return walk is uphill.

Walk from Pico do Arieiro to Pico Ruivo

This walk is the most spectacular on Madeira – and consequently one of the most popular. Unless you have arranged for someone to meet you at Achada do Teixeira, at the other end, you'll need to allow around five to six hours (11km) for a tough return trip. Alternatively, consider taking one of the numerous organized walks (see p.198), which include pick-ups at Pico Ruivo.

It's best to set off early to get the best views and be free of crowds. Although there are some pretty scary drops at times, the walk is easily manageable if you take sensible precautions, wear good boots and take a torch.

The clearly signed path heads off from Pico do Arieiro's car park along a narrow spine of

▲ PENHA DA ÁGUIA FROM FAIAL

rock with drops to either side, though any steep parts are fenced off. The first stretch of this walk takes in some startling volcanic landscape, with basalt columns and sills rising like bones through the soft, reddish ferrous soil.

After around forty minutes the path splits. Stick to the left fork (the right-hand path is unstable); this descends some steps before passing through a series of short tunnels, the first of which goes under Pico do Gato. Once you're through the tunnel, ignore a gated path to the right and continue straight on. The next section, a fifteen-minute walk until the second tunnel, crosses a very steep drop with just a rather wobbly wire fence to protect you from the precipice. But there are plenty of mountain plants to take your mind off the drop, including tiny pink geraniums, and the weird interlocking leaves of the horse leeks.

Shortly after the second tunnel the path goes through a third, slightly longer, tunnel, soon followed by two shorter tunnels; after the fifth tunnel another path joins from the right, but

continue straight on. The path winds past ancient, 200-year-old heather trees and you'll also see some caves, which shepherds use for shelter. You then climb quite steeply; here the contorted, bleached white branches of the heather trees are intertwined along the edge of the path to stabilize the soil against rock falls.

Two hours into the walk, you come to the Pico Ruivo government rest house, a lovely spot with trees all around (and a public toilet), where most tour groups rest for lunch. The summit of Pico Ruivo is a tantalizing climb above: the path is steep, but it only takes ten minutes to reach a viewing platform at the summit (see p.171).

At 1862m, this point has even more spectacular views than Pico do Arieiro (which you can see in the distance). From the summit, either return the way you came to Pico Arieiro (taking great care to follow the route in reverse and not to stray from the main path) or, if you have transport to collect you, head back down to the government rest house, from

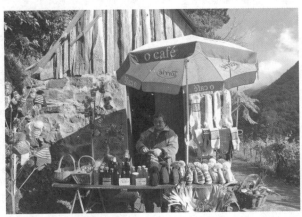

▲ CRAFT STALL NEAR BALCÕES

where the path continues for around 45 minutes northeast across a relatively flat ridge to Achada do Teixeira (see p.171).

Poiso and the Parque Ecológico do Funchal

São Gonçalo bus #103 or #138 (1 daily; 30min). The EN103 begins its descent to Funchal at **Poiso**, a 1400-metre mountain pass. Poiso means "resting place", as this was the traditional spot for travellers to stop when going from coast to coast. Many drivers still pause at the excellent *Casa de Abrigo* (see p.177).

The steep slopes to the west of Poiso form part of the **Parque Ecológico do Funchal**, a protected area used as an outdoor "education centre" for students. You'll see tracks into the park signed off the main Poiso–Funchal road. Inside the park, there are further marked paths, picnic tables and barbecue spots. Its steep slopes, fed by deep bedded water courses, create microclimates that are ideal for a variety of flora and bird life. A practised eye can spot indigenous Til trees, giant species of laurel such as Loureiro, Vinhático and Barbusano, and birds such as the Manx shearwater, sparrowhawks, red-legged partridges, barn owls, Madeiran robins, blackcaps and firecrests.

Hotels

Cabanas

Sítio da Beira da Quinta (São Jorge) ☏291 576 291, ⓦwww.cabanasvillage .com. A tourist complex, 2km west of São Jorge, consisting of 25 circular bungalows, each of which sleeps up to two adults and a child. Some of

them lie close to the clifftop, with great views down the coast, though most of them are set back amid lawns. There's a mid-price restaurant, a tiny swimming pool, a craft shop and a bar, along with two re-created Santana houses next to the restaurant. The location is certainly impressive, but the huts – said to have been inspired by Zulu huts after the founder's stay in Africa – are too densely packed and gimmicky for a stay of more than one night. €60.

Casa de Capelinha

Terreiro, Ponta Delgada ☏291 860 040, ⓦwww.casadacapelinha.com. A stylish designer hotel with white, cubist rooms facing the sea. Neat modern decor and grounds which include a small pool, games room and little restaurant-bar. €50, not including breakfast.

O Colmo

Sítio do Serrado, Santana ☏291 570 290, ⓦwww.hotelcolmo.com. On the main road just up from the post office, this modern four-star hotel is built in traditional style, with decent-sized rooms, each with satellite TV. There's a big restaurant downstairs which often fills with tour groups. The heated indoor pool, gym and sauna make it all good value. €70.

Monte Mar Palace

Sítio do Montado, Ponta Delgada ☏291 860 030, ⓦmontemar-palace. com. A large, ungainly block, but wonderfully sited on a bluff just west of Ponta Delgada, popular with package companies. Comfy, if functional, rooms with balconies, air conditioning and large bathrooms. There's a so-so in-house restaurant, indoor and outdoor pools, spa, gym and

Northern and central Madeira **PLACES**

▲ COMPLEXO BALNEAR DE SÃO JORGE

even a little putting green. €90, including dinner.

Quinta do Arco

Arco de São Jorge ☎291 570 270, ⓦwww.quintadoarco.com. If you want to get away from it all, this complex of cottages sleeping up to four people is a perfect rural escape. Built in traditional style, with wooden stairs and rustic drapes, the cottages each have a living room and kitchenette, with a cosy upstairs bedroom. The grounds are gorgeous, with lush vegetation, an honesty bar and a small pool. €80.

Quinta Furão

Achada do Gramacho (Santana) ☎291 570 100, ⓦwww.quintadofurao .com. This large, modern three-storey hotel is spectacularly positioned in one of Madeira's largest vineyards (see p.167) on a clifftop some 4km west of Santana. The third-floor rooms have balconies with great views over the cliffs. There's also a heated pool and gym, and a restaurant, bar and shop in a separate building 50m down the hill (see opposite). €100.

Solar de Boaventura

Serrão Boaventura, Boaventura ☎291 860 888, ⓦwww. solar-boaventura. com. Very plush and imaginatively designed hotel set in a huge lawned area in a valley just off the road to Santana. The original *solar* (manor house) dates from 1776 and served as a school and medical centre before its current reincarnation as the hotel reception and pricey but excellent restaurant (daily 1–3pm & 7–10pm). The *solar* has a series of lavish modern extensions, comprising atriums, bedrooms and communal areas. All rooms have bathrooms and TVs. €60.

Restaurants

A Chave

Sítio da Igreja, Faial ☎291 573 262. Daily 10am–midnight. Situated opposite the church, this place does sizzlingly good fish and meat dishes at decent prices, and has a lovely terrace garden, complete with bird-of-paradise flowers, a small fish pond and distant sea views.

Complexo Balnear de São Jorge

Foz da Ribeira (São Jorge) ☏291 576 734. Daily 9am–2am. The little restaurant overlooking the sea pools at this lido serves excellent-value, generous portions of fish and dishes such as *arroz de marisco* (seafood rice) and *cozido* (stew) from around €5–6.

Piscina

Ponta Delgada ☏291 862 400. Mon–Thurs & Sun 10am–7pm, Fri & Sat 10am–9pm. A stylish bar-restaurant with groovy coloured plastic seats facing the sea pools. The inexpensive menu features reliably tasty omelettes and fish such as *bodião* (parrot fish) and salmon from around €10. The bar offers cheap beer with *tremoços*, pickled lupin seeds.

Quinta Furão

Achada do Gramacho (Santana) ☏291 570 100. Daily noon–3.30pm & 7–9.30pm. Reservations are advised for a meal at this fine place, just below the hotel of the same name (see opposite), 4km west of Santana. The slightly formal restaurant offers expensive, but unusual, dishes from around €12, such as steak *a caldeirão verde* (with pastry and roquefort) and desserts such as ice cream with wild fruits. Vegetarian dishes include grilled vegetables with Santana cheese, and there's an extensive wine list. There's a superb view over the cliffs from the front terrace.

Victor's

Ribeiro Frio ☏291 575 898. Daily 9am–6pm. Cosy, wood-lined café-restaurant with a log fire; the reasonable menu offers trout from the local farm, as well as grilled meats, pasta and salads; also mid-priced drinks and snacks.

Café-bars

1958

São Jorge. Mon–Fri 7am–1pm & 2–10pm, Sat 7am–1pm. Right by the church, this supermarket-cum-café-bar sees most of the villagers at some point in the day; they pop in for supplies and a swift coffee or drink at a great little stand-up counter.

Casa de Abrigo

Poiso ☏291 782 269. Daily 8am–midnight. A popular mountain café-restaurant, usually smelling deliciously of wood smoke from its roaring fire. Mid-priced specialities include succulent roasted meats, including rich *cozido* stews, though many people get no further than having a *poncha* or two at the bar.

PLACES

Northern and central Madeira

▲ RIBEIRO FRIO TROUT FARM

Porto Santo

The small island of Porto Santo, just 11km long and 6km wide, lies around 75km northeast of Madeira. It's relatively flat and arid with a long swathe of pristine sandy beach attracting droves of summer visitors from Madeira, but it's little visited at other times and remains one of Europe's least discovered beach destinations. Most of the island's five thousand inhabitants live in and around Vila Baleira, the attractive capital where Cristopher Columbus lived for a while. Porto Santo also claims one of the best golf courses in Portugal.

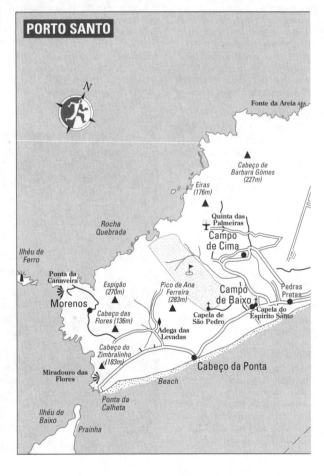

PORTO SANTO

Visiting Porto Santo

The **tourist office** is in Vila Baleira on Avenida Henrique Vieira de Castro 5 (Mon–Fri 9.30am–12.30pm & 2–5.30pm, ☎291 982 361), just off the main square. There are **banks** with ATMs at the bottom end of Avenida Henrique Vieira de Castro 5. You can access the **Internet** at Ciber Nauta, at Edifício Ilha Dourada, Vila Baleira ☎291 984 958 (daily 8am–2am).

Vila Baleira

With its largely sixteenth- and seventeenth-century architecture, red terracotta roofs, cobbled streets and exotic plants, Vila Baleira is as picturesque and lively a village as any on Madeira. The leafy and pedestrianized Avenida Infante Dom Henrique lures you down to its pristine Blue Flag beach. Though the town stretch inevitably is the busiest on the island, crowds are rarely

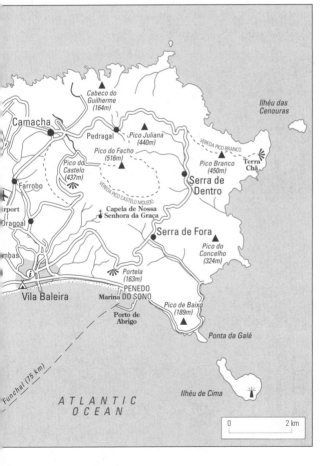

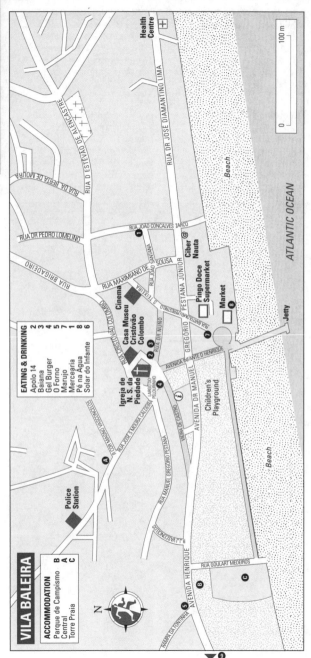

VILA BALEIRA

ACCOMMODATION
Parque de Campismo B
Central A
Torre Praia C

EATING & DRINKING
Apolo 14   2
Baiana   3
Gel Burger   4
O Forno   5
Marujo   7
Mercearia   1
Pé na Água   8
Solar do Infante   6

A brief history of Porto Santo

Geographically far older than Madeira, Porto Santo was discovered by the Portuguese explorers Zarco and Teixeira in 1418. They docked in its sheltered waters before setting off to explore the more forbidding-looking island of Madeira in the distance. Portuguese colonizers – mainly farmers and fishermen from southern Portugal – settled on Porto Santo from 1420. They planted vines and sugar cane and exploited the native dragon trees for their sap, which could be made into dye. The island's first governor was Bartolomeu Perestrelo, of Genoese ancestry, a friend of Christopher Columbus, who frequently visited the island in the late 1470s.

Unlike its sister island, Porto Santo never really prospered. The dragon trees were quickly felled and crops were decimated by imported rabbits, and between the fifteenth and the eighteenth centuries, Moorish, French and English pirates looted the low-lying, broad coastline more or less at will.

The opening of the airport, partly as a NATO base, in 1960, was a major boost to the economy, and today the island is increasingly dependent on tourism – which is just as well, as drought and deforestation have all but destroyed the island's agriculture.

PLACES Porto Santo

overwhelming. The soft sand on Porto Santo is said to have healing properties, ideal for those with eczema, varicose veins or an excess of city living, and elderly folk can often be seen lying buried up to their neck.

Lined with benches, the town jetty is a popular spot for evening walks and young lovers. Just by the entrance to the jetty is the town's little market building and a statue of a Barqueiro, a traditional boatman.

It's a short walk to the palm-shaded main square, the highly attractive Largo do Pelourinho, containing the village's squat, two-tiered Câmara Municipal (town hall), flanked by sentry-like dragon trees. Adjacent is the white seventeenth-century Igreja de Nossa Senhora da Piedade, built on the site of Vila Baleira's original church, destroyed by pirates in 1667. A decorative *azulejos* panel adorns the exterior, and there are further *azulejos* inside.

Vila Baleira: Casa Museu Cristóvão Colombo

Rua Cristóvão Colombo 12. Tues–Fri 10am–12.30 & 2–5.30pm; July–Sept

also open Sun 10am–1pm. Free. The island's most famous building, the Casa Museu Cristóvão Colombo was once the home of Christopher Columbus (see box on p.182). Now heavily restored, it comprises an attractive series of rooms displaying artefacts either connected with Columbus or related to the history of the island. There are various portraits of the great man and scenes from his adventures, together with maps of his journeys and models of the boats he sailed in. The last room, just off the central courtyard, contains two sunken grain stores along with treasures

▲ TOWN HALL, VILA BALEIRA

Christopher Columbus

Christopher Columbus's links with Porto Santo began in 1478 when he visited the island while working for a Genoese sugar merchant based in Lisbon. He may have been visiting fellow Genoese Bartolomeu Perestrelo, Porto Santo's first governor, or exploring the possibilities of exporting sap from the island's dragon trees. He was soon to return, for in 1479 he married Filipa Moniz, Bartolomeu Perestrelo's daughter, whom he met after a church service in Machico in Madeira. It is thought that they lived on Porto Santo until 1484, in the house which is now Vila Baleira's Columbus Museum. In 1484, they moved to Funchal, where not long afterwards Filipa died giving birth to their son.

During his time on Porto Santo, it is said that Columbus was inspired to set off for America after seeing seeds and wood washed up on Porto Santo's beach, making him wonder if there were land further west. He asked the court in Lisbon to sponsor his explorations, but was refused any help. In 1485, Spain agreed to back his journey, and in 1492 he set off from Palos, landing on the American continent three months later, though at the time he was convinced he had discovered a western sea route to India.

The island celebrates the explorer with an annual **Christopher Columbus Week** in late September. The five-day festival consists of re-enactments of Columbus's landing on Porto Santo in a replica boat, a mock wedding ceremony of the kind that Columbus and Filipa Moniz would have gone through, period musical performances, flag ceremonies and a medieval market.

retrieved from the *Carrock*, a Dutch boat owned by the East India Company which sank off the north coast of Porto Santo in 1724 en route to Jakarta. The ship went down with most of its crew, boxes of silver ingots, Spanish and Dutch coins and valuable ceramics.

Campo de Baixo and around

Buses #4 & #7 from Vila Baleira (7–10 daily). Around 4km west of Vila Baleira lies the village of Campo de Baixo. It boasts a beautiful church, the elegantly fading pink-fronted eighteenth-century Capela do Espírito Santo, built when the village was an important farming community – Campo de Baixo means "lower field". Today the sprawling village relies on a handful of shops, cafés and hotels that have grown up a short walk from the superb wide stretch of soft sandy beach.

It is also a short walk from a new tennis centre and the southern fringes of Porto Santo's golf course (see p.184). A dirt track just west of the course heads up to a viewpoint on the wind-eroded slopes of Pico de

▲ THE JETTY, VILA BALEIRA

▲ PORTO SANTO

Ana Ferreira (283m), a conical volcanic peak.

Cabeço da Ponta

Bus #4 & #7 from Vila Baleira (7–10 daily). Three kilometres west of Campo de Baixa lies Cabeço da Ponta, consisting of a small cluster of apartments, restaurants and two large hotels just back from the island's widest, most exhilarating part of the beach. It makes a great spot for a beach holiday away from it all, though after dark your options for eating and entertainment are somewhat limited. This may change before long, though, as the stretch between Campo de Baixo and Cabeço da Ponta is earmarked for several tourist developments, including a casino, but for the time being the only nightlife consists of the giant moths that flutter round the hotel lights.

Ponta da Calheta

Bus #4 from Vila Baleira via Campo de Baixo and Cabeço da Ponta (4–8 daily). West of Cabeço da Ponta, the beach, backed by steep dunes, gets quieter and more rugged. At Ponta da Calheta, the sand gives way to volcanic rock sculpted by the elements into wonderfully shaped arches and blowholes. The only building in Ponta da Calheta is the *Calhetas* restaurant (see p.189), a great spot to watch the sun set on the horizon beside the distant outline of Madeira.

Northwestern Porto Santo

Just off the main road, past Porto Santo's Centro Hipico (riding centre) a left turn takes you to **Miradouro das Flores**, a viewpoint right above Ponta da Calheta offering the island's most spectacular views: you can see right along the length of the beach one way and the island of Madeira the other. The dusty viewpoint is marked by a statue of deaf Portuguese painter Francisco Maya, a twentieth-century eccentric who loved to paint Porto Santo and asked to be buried at sea between this point and the offshore islet of Ilhéu de Ferro.

The dirt road continues north to **Morenos**, a hilltop picnic spot neatly laid out with wooden tables, barbecue grills

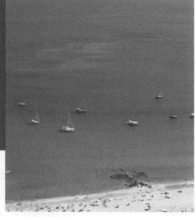

▲ PORTO SANTO BEACH

contrast to the arid landscape around it, and the design is heavily influenced by the desert-like environs. The clubhouse is a modern medley of stone, glass and bamboo punctuated with neatly potted cacti. The course itself bends round water features and is all cambers and slopes. Beginners are not allowed onto the course, though you can take thirty-minute lessons (Wed–Sun) from €15.

and fresh-water taps. Apart from weekends in summer, when locals descend in droves, the place is usually deserted.

Porto Santo Golf

℗291 983 778, @www.Madeira-golf .com. The brainchild of Spanish golfing supremo Severiano Ballesteros, the Porto Santo golf course is both larger and more challenging than the courses on Madeira. Its greens and fairways stand out in vivid

Quinta das Palmeiras

Daily: May–Sept 9am–7pm; Oct–April 10am–1pm & 3–5pm. €2. Plonked in the middle of one of the most barren parts of the island, Quinta das Palmeiras is a little oasis of greenery, a privately run mini-botanical garden consisting of fruit trees, vines and exotic plants. Imaginatively landscaped paths run past cages of peacocks, love birds, toucans, parrots and finches to a duck pond complete with swans, just

▼ PORTO SANTO'S SANDY BEACH

below a café. There is even an impressively large rhea. Buses don't call here, but island tours visit, or you could splash out on a taxi from your hotel.

Camacha and Fonte da Areia

Bus #1 from Vila Baleira (2–3 daily). The main settlement in the north, Camacha consists of a sprawl of white houses set on a barren slope overlooking the rocky coast. The only local sight is Fonte da Areia, the "spring of the sands", once Camacha's main water supply. The water is said to have healing powers, and for a time it was bottled and sold to Madeira and mainland Portugal, but the process became uneconomic. A series of stone huts and palm trees have grown up round the spring, a tranquil spot for a picnic. A marked trail winds steeply down a cliff to a wave-battered sandy beach – a pleasant, if tiring, thirty-minute return walk.

Pico do Castelo and Pedragal

The picturesque wooded peak of **Pico do Castelo**, at 437m the fourth highest on the island, towers over the island. Reached on a rough, cobbled track, a cacti-lined *miradouro* offers great views of the airport and both north and south coasts. A rusting cannon is the only one that remains of the twelve that once circled the mountain, part of the seventeenth-century

fortifications installed to keep the Spanish at bay during their occupation of Portugal from 1581 to 1640. From the *miradouro* a path climbs to the summit of the mountain, and then continues all the way to **Pedragal**, an abandoned farm, on the main north-coast road. However, if you fancy walking the entire route – it takes around two hours – it's best to do it in reverse to avoid ending your walk in the middle of nowhere. You could easily get a taxi to Pedragal, for example, and after your walk take a bus or taxi from Camacha back to your hotel. From Pedragal the walk to Pico do Castelo is clearly signposted, though it is a tough climb, circling the cedar-topped peaks of Pico da Gandaia and Pico do Facho en route. From Pico do Castelo, however, it is a relatively easy descent to Camacha.

Terra Chã and Pico Branco

A couple of kilometres east of Pedragal lies the start of a signed mountain walk to the lookout point of Terra Chã via Pico Branco. It's a four-kilometre return trek and takes

▲ PICO DO CASTELO

Porto Santo PLACES

▲ THE WALK TO TERRA CHÃ

two to three hours. Perhaps the best walk on the island, it's relatively easy and takes in a diverse landscape, from desert-like scrub to woodland, with excellent views all the way. The path takes you up the steep, barren slopes of Pico Branco. As you approach the top of the 450-metre-high mountain the scenery becomes greener and wooded. The mountain provides refuge to a rare species of giant snail that was once common. From here the path continues to Terra Chã, the northeastern tip of the island, from where there are superb views of Ilhéu das Cenouras to the east.

Serra de Dentro and Portela

Bus #2 from Vila Baleira (Mon–Fri 3–4 daily). The deep Serra de Dentro valley was once prime agricultural land, but over the years, owing to drought, this has given way to row upon row of deserted, terraced slopes, leaving the tiny village of **Serra de Dentro** as a ghost town of eerily decaying houses and farm buildings. The valley, however, is a good place to spot rare birds, including kestrels, falcons and crested hoopoes.

A kilometre south, the road swings round to the *miradouro* at **Portela**, a superb viewpoint, looking over the beach and harbour below, backed by a row of old traditional windmills.

Beyond here, on a blowy ridge, you'll see the hilltop Capela de Nossa Senhora da Graça, parts of which date back to the fifteenth century, making it one of the oldest churches on the island.

Hotels

Residencial Central

Rua C. Magno Vasconcelos, Vila Baleira ☏291 982 226, ⊕291 983 460. This modern, white, low-rise *residencial* on a hill five minutes' walk from the centre is the best-value budget option in town. Rooms are spotless and include en-suite bathrooms and TVs. There are sweeping sea views from the upper rooms and the small, leafy terrace. Facilities include a bar and large breakfast room. €56.

Luamar Aparthotel

Cabeço da Ponta ☏291 984 121, ⊛www.torrepraia.pt. This low-rise hotel, set on a wide, sandy beach, is ideal for families and self-caterers. Though slightly showing their age, the compact, well-designed apartments (which sleep up to four people) come with living room, bathroom and kitchenette. It's worth paying extra to have an apartment facing the sea rather than the main road, and all rooms come with balconies or – for those on the ground floor – terraces opening up onto lawned areas. There's a large outdoor pool, a lunchtime café, mini-market, sauna, gym and a daytime courtesy bus to Vila Baleira. €114, or €138 with a sea view.

Hotel Porto Santo

Ribeiro Cochino, Campo do Baixo ☎291 980 140, ⍟www.hotelportosanto.com. The island's most sophisticated hotel, with antiques adding a formal air to a discreet, low-rise four-star set in its own palm-tree-studded lawns just back from the beach. The modestly sized rooms all have cable TV, air-conditioning and balconies facing the lawns or fields at the side. There's a restaurant and terrace facing the outdoor pool

with a separate children's pool. Other facilities include a crazy golf course, tennis courts and playground; the hotel can also arrange watersports, horse riding and bike rental. €120.

Hotel Torre Praia

Rua Goulart Madeiros, Vila Baleira ☎291 980 450, ⍟www.torrepraia .pt. A large, modern four-star hotel right on the beach in the west of town, imaginatively constructed round the stone tower (*torre*) of an old cement factory which dominates the reception area. The best rooms are those on the upper floors with sea views; lower ones overlook lawns to the side. There's a small pool, restaurant, squash court, gym, sauna, jacuzzi and direct access to the beach. The panoramic bar (daily from 9pm) offers fine views. €156.

Hotel Vila Baleira

Sítio do Cabeço da Ponta ☎291 980 800, ⍟www.vilabaleira.com. Located in Cabeço da Ponta, this pink high-rise hotel has 256 rooms and a separate annexe with 56 apartments. Both blocks are set back from the sea on the wrong side of the coastal highway

▲ SERRA DE DENTRO

▲ TRADITIONAL WINDMILL

and bizarrely skewed so that
none of the large, functional
rooms directly face the Atlantic.
Nevertheless, the international-
standard facilities are first-rate,
with an in-house restaurant,
indoor pool, shops, games room,
children's room and bar. A
tunnel under the road leads to
a highly rated thelassotherapy
centre (open to non-residents),
along with an open-air pool,
children's play area and a
restaurant (daily 11am–3.30pm)
for barbecued sardines, chicken
and pizzas. The hotel also lays
on live entertainment. €216.

Residencial Virgilio

Sítio do Espírito Santo, Campo do Baixo
☎291 980 110, ☎291 980 115. A
three-storeyed modern *residencial*
on the main south-coast
highway, some five minutes'
walk from the beach. Its good-
sized rooms are spotless and

come with balconies
and private bathrooms.
The complex includes
a dull restaurant
downstairs (daily
noon–3pm & 7–10pm),
offering moderately
priced Madeiran staples,
a decent café (daily
10am–10pm) and a
shop (daily 10am–2pm
& 5–9pm), selling
touristy handicrafts and
wine. €75, or €80 for
sea views.

Campsites

Parque de Campismo Porto Santo

Rua Goulart Madeiros, Vila
Baleira ☎291 983 111.
Porto Santo's only
campsite occupies
a spacious sandy
enclosure just off the
highway. Basic facilities include
a children's play area, cold
showers and limited shade in the
form of a few trees and bushes.

Cafés

Gel Burger

Largo do Pelourinho, Vila Baleira. Daily
8am–2am. With outside tables
sprawling out onto the main
square beneath palm trees, this
is the liveliest café in town,
offering everything from
morning coffee and croissants
to light meals, pastries, cakes, ice
creams and drinks. The counter
usually has a fine range of meat
and tuna rissoles.

Marujo

Praça do Barqueiro, Vila Baleira. Daily
8am–2am. Adjacent to the main
market, this modern, wood-
panelled café-bar has boppy

sounds and a great terrace facing the jetty; outside tables nestle under palm trees.

Tia Maria

Ribeira Salgado. Daily 11am–8pm. Right on the beach between Cabeço da Ponta and Campo de Baixo, this café-bar is built in traditional stone with an outdoor terrace facing the sands – a great spot for a snack or a sunset beer. It also does pricey meals in high season.

Restaurants

Baiana

Rua do Dr Nuno S. Teixeira 7, Vila Baleira ☎ 291 984 649. Daily 10am–2am. The best place in town for a full meal, this airy, wood-ceilinged restaurant just east of the main square is always busy. There are superb starters such as cheeses, olives and spongy garlic bread. Main courses are around €12 and include barbecued chicken, grilled prawns, *bife na pedra* (steak cooked on a stone) and *caldeirada* (stew). Fresh fish usually includes *bodião* (parrot fish), *badejo* (coal fish) and octopus. Leave room for the tasty desserts and milkshakes.

O Calhetas

Calheta ☎ 291 984 380. Daily noon–10pm. With a smart, minimalist interior, this bar-restaurant offers the best – and priciest – beachside food on the island, with an outdoor terrace offering great views over Ilhéu de Baixo and the distant outline of Madeira. There are a few meat dishes, though it is best known for its fresh fish and seafood such as *caldeirada* (fish casserole). Full meals run to about €18 a head, but you don't have to splash; the attached bar does

drinks, ice creams and snacks such as octopus sandwiches. Phone ahead and the restaurant will pick you up from your hotel and drive you back again afterwards.

Estrela do Norte

Sítio da Camacha, Camacha ☎ 291 983 500. Daily 10am–4pm & 7pm–2am. People from all over the island visit this highly rated *churrascaria* for its superior, if slightly pricey, grilled meat and fish served in a modern, barn-like, stone-clad room with wooden benches. There are a few outdoor seats on a gravel forecourt or under a covered porch.

O Forno

Rampa da Fontinha, Vila Baleira ☎ 291 985 141. Daily 11am–11pm. Bustling, good-value place with a modern decor of wood and chrome tables and chairs, offering traditional barbecue-grilled *espetada*, and meats, along with home-baked bread. Plain and simply grilled chicken is often the best bet at around €9. The entrance is opposite the campsite on the main south coast road.

Mar e Sol

Estrada do Forno da Cal, Campo de Baixo ☎ 291 982 269. Daily except Tues 10am–midnight. A traditional-style restaurant with an outdoor terrace on a raised bit of dune, overlooking a wide swathe of beach. Moderately priced specialities include tuna steaks, *fragateira* (fish stew) and other fish dishes. The speciality is *feijoada* (bean stew) for two for €30.

Mercearia

Rua João Santana 26, Vila Baleira ☎ 291 982 580. Mon–Sat 11am–3pm & 8pm–midnight. With a bar area full of wine barrels and an attractive patio with tables under the palms, this is a characterful place for inexpensive thin-crust pizzas, fine salads, toasts and pasta dishes. Also offers Internet access.

Pé na Água
Rua das Pedras Pretos, Pedras Pretos ☏291 983 114. Daily 11am–11pm. Just out of Vila Baleira, the "foot in the water" is an arty restaurant which blends modern design with a rustic beach look. Food and service are first rate, with mid-priced fish and seafood, including *arroz de marisco* or *cataplana* for two for €30. There are outside seats on decking facing the beach.

Solar do Infante
Praça do Barqueiro, Vila Baleira ☏291 985 279. Daily noon–midnight. A swish, stone-clad restaurant right by the jetty, with wooden floors and a sleek glass and steel interior. Service is slick but prices reasonable for such well prepared dishes as *arroz de marisco* and *tamboril* (monkfish) for two for around €22. The outside terrace has great views over the beach.

Bars

Apolo 14
Rua do Dr Nuno S. Teixeira 3–5, Vila Baleira. Daily 9am–midnight. Locals prop up the bar in this small bar-restaurant on the main square, with Coral beer on tap and walls lined with crusty bottles of wine; and families also pop in for coffee, ice creams or inexpensive meals served at a couple of indoor tables or out on the square. It also serves vinho do Porto Santo, the local, sherry-like wine.

João do Cabeço
Sítio do Cabeço, Cabeço da Ponta. Daily 6pm–1am. On the main road between the Luamar and the Hotel Vila Baleira, this traditional stone building with a clay roof attracts a young clientele for drinks, toasts and snacks such as *chouriço* (sausage), *picado* (garlicky beef), *pregos* (beef in a roll) and *camarão* (shrimps). Rock and pop music inside and a covered terrace outside.

PXO
Sítio da Camacha, Camacha. Daily 10am–10pm. This small bar-restaurant does a fine range of *doces* (tapas-style snacks) such as *calamares*, octopus and *chouriço* sausage, along with full meals for €10–13. At weekends there is usually live music, from fado to crooning Karaoke singers.

Clubs

Challenger Beach
Penedo do Sono. Daily 10pm–8am. The harbourside branch of Vila Baleira's main club has taken over as the place to go on the island, with dance sounds till dawn and a mean range of drinks including *batidinhas* (fruit shakes) and *caipirinhas* (Brazilian cane-juice cocktails).

Colombo's Sports Bar
Penedo do Sono. Daily 10pm–8am. With a groovy curved bar and an upstairs terrace, this is one of the best positioned of the row of warehouse-style bars and clubs facing the harbour. Lively sounds and a friendly crowd that picks up after midnight.

Essentials

Arrival

Most visitors arrive at Madeira airport, some 18km to the east of the capital, Funchal. There are regular connections from the airport to Porto Santo (see below).

Madeira

If you're arriving on a package then you'll probably have a free transfer to your hotel from the airport. Otherwise, the Aerobus (roughly hourly 10am–11.30pm, return 9am–10pm; €4, free to TAP passengers; 25min) runs to Funchal's seafront and into the Hotel Zone. Local SAM **buses** #20, #53, #78, #156 also do the run but take up to twice as long. The SAM bus terminal is on Avenida Calouste Gulbenkian, from where it's just ten minutes' walk to the tourist office (see p.196). A **taxi** from the airport to Funchal takes twenty minutes and costs €20–30.

By **car**, take the fast airport road, which skirts round the northern upper slopes of the city and follow signs to central Funchal (signed *Centro*). For the Hotel Zone, follow signs to *Funchal Oeste*.

Porto Santo

Regular fifteen-minute TAP Air Portugal **flights** from Madeira airport operate every one to two hours (☎291 520 821; ⓦ www.tap-airportugal.pt, €120–125 return). There are no buses from Porto Santo's airport, but plenty of taxis and you'll only pay about €5 for the ten-minute trip into Vila Baleira, the capital.

The Porto Santo Ferry Line (☎291 982 543, ⓦ www.portosantoline.pt) runs a daily **ferry** from Funchal harbour to Porto de Abrigo (Sun–Thurs 8am, Fri 7pm; no Tues sailings Jan–May & Oct–Dec; €60 return; 2hr 30min). Arrive at the ferry terminal at least thirty minutes before departure. Large items of luggage can be left on the numbered palettes next to the ferry entrance; remember the number and retrieve the luggage yourself at the other end. Connecting buses to Vila Baleira take five minutes (€1), while a taxi costs around €4. Ferries return to Funchal Mon & Wed–Sat at 6pm, Tues at 9pm, Sun 7pm (no Tues sailings in Jan–May & Oct–Dec).

You can also visit the island on a day-trip "cruise", with return prices at €52 (Oct–April) or €60 (May–Sept).

Transport

Madeira and Porto Santo have an efficient bus network and taxis are a relatively inexpensive option. But if you're planning to get off the beaten track, you're going to have to rent a car, or rely on one of various tours.

Madeira

Although distances on the island are short, many of the roads are narrow and winding, so journeys can take time; nevertheless, even Porto Moniz, at the furthest point of the island, is less than two hours from Funchal.

Buses

Madeira's **buses** serve almost every village on the island from Funchal's various privately run bus terminals. **Tickets** are inexpensive – a ride from Funchal to Porto Moniz, in the far northeast of the island, costs around €5. For all journeys, tickets can be bought on board from the conductor.

Though reliable, the buses are geared to the needs of local people, so that day-trips are not always feasible. It's also worth noting that the buses don't serve much of the island's best scenic and walking territory, so it is probably worth considering car rental at some stage. Details of **buses from Funchal** to specific places on the island are given in the guide at the start of each account. From villages outside Funchal, look for timetables at bus stops marked *paragem*, or ask in the local café.

Car rental

Madeira's size means that nowhere is too far to visit on a day-trip from Funchal by **car**. An ambitious EU-funded tunnelling programme has greatly reduced journey times with a network of underground dual carriageways, though try and take some of the old, winding roads for a chance to see more of the landscape. It's worth getting hold of a good map, however, as road signs are biased in favour of the new highway.

Rental prices are reasonable. Expect to pay around €30–40 a day or €200–250 a week. Third-party insurance is usually included in the price, though further insurance is recommended to avoid hefty excess charges for damages. Petrol is subsidized at around €1 a litre.

To rent a car, you'll need a current driving licence from your home country or an international driving licence – as well as your passport – which you must have with you at all times when driving.

Car parking is easy outside Funchal; in Funchal itself it's best to head to a central car park. In other towns it is usually easy to find a pay-and-display bay. Prices for these start at around €0.50 an hour, usually on *dias utéis* (weekdays) only.

Car rental companies

Atlantic-Rent-a-Car Centro Comercial Belo Sol, Caminho Velho Ajuda, Funchal ☏291 765 208.

Atlas Av Infante 29, Funchal ☏291 223 100, ☏291 741 212.

Avis Largo António Nobre 164, Funchal ☏291 764 546; *Hotel Monumental Lido*, Funchal ☏291 764 546; airport ☏291 524 392, ☏www.avis.com.

Bravacar Caminho do Amparo 2, Funchal ☏291 764 400.

Budget *Hotel Duas Torres*, Estrada Monumental 239, Funchal ☏291 766 518; airport ☏291 524 661, ☏www.budget.com.

Hertz Centro Comercial Monumental Lido Loja 1, Estrada Monumental, Funchal ☏291 764 410; airport ☏291 523 040, ☏www.hertz.com.

Lidorent Edifício Alto Lido, Estrada Monumental, Funchal ☏291 761 420, ☏291 761 635.

Moinho Estrada Monumental 28, Funchal ☏291 762 123, ☏291 766 188.

Rent-a-car do Futuro Centro Comercial Infante, Loja G, Avda Do Infante, Funchal ☏291 220 721.

Rodavente Edifício Baía, Estrada Monumental, Funchal ☏291 758 506; airport ☏291 524 718.

Sixt Estrada Monumental 182, Funchal ☏291 764 221, ☏www.e-sixt.com.

Bus companies

Buses in and around Funchal are served by the yellow **Horários do Funchal** (☏291 705 555). Generally the west and northwest of the island is served by **Rodoeste Buses** (☏291 233 830), which leave from Rua Ribeira João Gomes, Funchal. The east and northeast of the island, including the airport, is served by **SAM Buses** (☏291 706 710) from Rua Calouste Gulbenkian, Funchal. Three smaller companies – **Empresa de Automóveis do Caniço** (to Caniço; ☏291 222 558); **Companhia dos Carros de São Gonçalo** (to Camacha, Santo do Serra, the north and Curral das Freiras; ☏291 923 877); and **São Roque do Faial** (to the north coast via Ribeiro Frio; ☏291 220 060) – all have their terminals on the Zona Velha end of Avenida do Mar in Funchal.

Taxis

If you don't fancy driving yourself, it is worth considering hiring a **taxi** for a day or half-day tour to any part of the island, or for local runs (to the start of walks, for example). Most authorized taxi drivers speak good English and they can be extremely knowledgeable as guides. The tourist office in Funchal can book taxi tours in advance at set rates. If you want to book your own driver, call ☎91 873 6563. Make sure you agree a price beforehand. Prices start at around €45 for a half day, €85 for a full day.

Motorbikes

Motorbikes are an excellent way of getting round the island and the narrow streets of central Funchal, though you'll need to rent a machine of above 100cc to be able to negotiate the mountainous interior. Prices start at around €11 a day. You'll need to be over 21, hold a valid **driving licence** from your home country or an international driving licence, and your passport. You must keep these at all times when you are driving. A hefty security deposit is also usually required. Wearing a **helmet** is obligatory; these come as part of the bike rental. Try **Joyride** (Centro Comercial Olimpo, Loja 210, Avenida do Infante, Funchal ☎291 234 906, ⓦwww.madeiramotorbikes.com), which also rents out mountain bikes.

Tours

Most major hotels and travel agents can arrange well-organized and informative island-wide **sightseeing coach tours**, usually with a daily changing programme. Good value is Strawberry World, Centro Comercial Monumental Lido, Estrada Monumental, Funchal ☎291 762 429, ⓦwww.strawberry-world.com.

A more dramatic, if pricey, way of seeing the spectacular scenery of the island is to take a **helicopter tour**. HeliAtlantis (☎291 232 882, ⓦwww.viator.com) rides depart from just below Parque da Santa Catarina in Funchal, for €55 (for 10min) or €72 (for 15min).

In Funchal, Carristur (☎968 342 413) offers hop-on hop-off open-top **bus** tours of the town (daily every 30min 10am–2.30pm & 3.30–5.30pm; €7.50), taking in most of the main sights.

Porto Santo

Six **bus** routes, operated by Horários de Transportes, run round the island serving most sights – details are given in the text – but they are geared up to the needs of local people rather than tourists, so you may have to hang around for return buses. **Taxis** are relatively inexpensive; a ride from one end of the island to the other costs no more than €18, except during weekends and at night when tariffs double. The main taxi rank in Vila Baleira is on Rua Dr Nuno Silvestre Teixeira (☎291 982 334).

Car rental is available at the airport from Moinho, (☎291 982 780 or ☎291 291 983 260, ⓦwww.moinho-rentacar .com) from around €40 a day. You can rent scooters from Acessórios Colombo, near the campsite on Avenida Henrique Vieira de Castro, Vila Baleira (☎291 984 438) for around €20 a day, or bikes from €10 a day. They are a good way of getting up and down the flat coast road; bicycles are also rented out to non-residents by all the large hotels.

A slower but more traditional form of transport is the covered **carriola**, a colourful pony and trap that can be hired from the harbour or on the junction of Avenida Dr Manuel Gregório Pestana Júnior and Avenida Infante Dom Henrique in Vila Baleira. Half-hour rides start from €20.

Tours

An open-top bus, run by Moinho (☎291 982 780), does a daily 2.5-hour circuit of the island all year-round, leaving at 2pm from the petrol station outside the Pingo Doce in Vila Baleira (minimum of five people; €7 per person). Dunas (☎291 983 088, ⓔdunastravel@mail.telepac.pt) also offers island tours (3hr) from €15 per person, along with jeep safaris from €20; boat trips from €30 (minimum of four people); and walks, usually to the western peaks, from €15.

Accommodation

Madeira has some of the best-equipped **hotels** in the world: the majority of hotels are four-star rated and over, with page-long lists of facilities. Even three-star hotels often have swimming pools, restaurants and live entertainment. Package holidays are usually cheaper if you want a top-end hotel, but if you are travelling independently, you'll find a good range of options, from hotels and guesthouses (called a *pensão* or *residencial*) to rural *quintas*, or manor houses. Villas are relatively scarce, though self-catering rooms with kitchenettes are available at many of the bigger hotels. **Camping** is limited to one site in the north (see p.161) and another on Porto Santo (see p.188), though it's possible to camp in restricted areas with prior permission; ⓦ www .madeira-camping.com can arrange this.

In the guide we give **prices** for the cheapest double room at peak-season summer rates, though at New Year rates rocket and a minimum stay may be required: it is best to book well in advance over this period. Most hotels offer a fifty-percent reduction for children aged 2–12, and under-2s are usually free.

Unless otherwise stated, all the places listed have breakfast included in the price.

Quintas, inns, country houses and rooms

Before *Reid's* became Funchal's first purpose-built hotel, visitors to the island were put up at wealthy landowners' country manors, known as **quintas**. Nowadays many of these *quintas* have been adapted to offer characterful, hotel-style accommodation once more, sometimes in the original buildings or in modern extensions. Again, amenities tend to be first rate, with many having pools, lush grounds and self-catering facilities.

Away from Funchal and the main towns you can also find quality accommodation in rural areas in **estalagems** or **albergarias** – literally "inns" – which have similar facilities to *quintas*, usually with restaurants attached. Another option is staying in farms or country houses on a bed-and-breakfast basis – **Turismo no Espaço Rural** or **casas rural** (ⓦwww. madeira-rural.com); most offer meals and some have self-catering facilities.

In many of Madeira's smaller towns you will see signs advertising **quartos** or **dormidas** – private rooms in people's houses, which can also be good value, though most do not offer breakfast. Try asking at the local café.

Information

The main Madeira tourist office is in Funchal on Avenida Arriaga 16 (Mon–Fri 9am–8pm, Sat & Sun 9am–6pm; ☎291 211 902) Tourist offices throughout the island (listed in the guide) and most major hotels give out free **maps** of Madeira and the main towns, which are adequate for basic touring. For in-depth exploration, the best road map is the GeoCentre's 1:75,000 *Holiday Map, Madeira*, which includes Porto Santo, although even this may not show the newest sections of Madeira's ongoing road-building programme.

Most **European newspapers** arrive in Madeira on the day of publication. For upcoming events, try and get hold of *Agenda Cultural*, an excellent monthly listings magazine available from the tourist office and some hotels.

Madeira on the net

ⓦwww.madeiraonline.com. The main Madeira search engine, with links to countless other sites covering everything from walks to news, recipes, arts and education.

ⓦwww.madeira-portugal.com. Website promoting hotels on Madeira, with details of facilities and prices and pictures of the hotels themselves. Also car rental and tours.

ⓦwww.madeira-holiday.com. Well-designed and highly readable Net magazine run by the newspaper *Madeira Life*, with local news, features, good links and practical details.

ⓦwww.madeiratourism.org. The snazzy official tourist board site, offering general information and hotel contact details.

ⓦwww.madeira-island.com. Lively Net magazine with stacks of information on local news and events as well as details of accommodation, shops, car rental, etc.

ⓦwww.Madeira-real-estate.com. Where to go to buy up a slice of the island.

ⓦwww.madeira-shopping.com. Chance to buy Madeiran produce online, with everything from books, guide books and maps to cakes, CDs and wine.

ⓦwww.madinfo.pt. Portuguese site with information on everything from culture and news to travel and tourism.

Money

As many products need to be imported, Madeira is more expensive than mainland Portugal, but food, drink and entry to sights remain relatively inexpensive.

The currency is the **euro** (€). The easiest way to get money is to use a credit or debit card to withdraw cash from any of the large number of ATMs (signed *Multibanco*) found throughout the island. Any card using the Cirrus or Eurocheque system will work, as will all major credit cards (Visa, American Express, Mastercard and Eurocard). Credit and charge cards levy a fee of around three to four percent on any cash advance or purchase; for debit cards there is a small currency conversion fee and some banks also charge per transaction. Credit cards are accepted for payment in most hotels and restaurants.

It is very expensive to change **travellers' cheques**, although it is probably worth taking a supply in case your credit card is lost. Normal **banking hours** are Mon–Fri 8.30am–3pm. In Funchal, some banks also open Sat 9am–1pm. Currency exchange bureaux (*cambios*) generally open Mon–Fri 9am–1pm & 2–7pm, Sat 9am–7pm. Outside these hours, most major hotels offer currency exchange, though not always at favourable rates.

Food

Madeira does not share the culinary heritage of mainland Portugal, traditionally relying on limited local produce: namely maize, chicken, beef and the deep-sea fish, *espada* which can all make satisfying meals. Most restaurants also serve a range of well-prepared international dishes, while Italian, Chinese and Indian restaurants can be found throughout Funchal.

Menus generally appear in Portuguese with an English translation (see also the menu glossary, p.209). Most restaurants **open** for lunch from around noon until 3pm and for dinner from around 7pm to 11pm. Some close one day during the week.

Sports and leisure

With its wide open spaces and extensive coastline, Madeira is perfect for outdoor enthusiasts year-round, and there are countless activities that can be enjoyed either individually or as part of a group.

Walking

Some of the best walks on the island are detailed in this guide. These were accurate when the book went to press, but conditions change – landslides during the winter months can wipe out sections of path, as can road-building – so check that the walk is still manageable with the local tourist office or your hotel before you set off.

The best walking months are usually July, August and early September, when rain is unlikely and skies are generally clear – and high up, at least, it is not too hot. June is the month most likely to have cloud covering the coasts, while the rainier months can make levada paths slippery. At other times, clouds often form over the mountains in the afternoons, so an early start is the best option.

All the walks in this guide can be tackled by anyone who is averagely fit, but make sure you're properly prepared. Some paths cross precipitous terrain and weather conditions can change quickly, reducing visibility and making the paths extremely slippery. Always wear suitable footwear and take a torch, suncream and waterproofs.

If you are unsure about setting off on a walk alone, consider taking a **guided walk**. Most hotels organize a weekly walking programme, and the companies listed below offer half- or full-day walks, with prices starting at around €20 for a half day to €30–35 for full day tours. The price includes pick up and drop off at your hotel.

Levadas

The most famous walking trails on Madeira are the **levadas** – irrigation canals constructed to channel water from the mountains to lower-lying agricultural land. Some of the *levadas* have been hacked into the side of sheer-sided slopes, and they often run through tunnels. Initially the work was done by slaves imported from Portugal's former colonies in Africa; nowadays high-tech machinery does the job. They have been constructed with an astonishing degree of engineering accuracy, along carefully plotted gradients so that the water flows gently down to where it is needed. Water flow is carefully regulated by a system of sluices operated by the *levadeiros* – men whose job it is to ensure that different farmers get an equal amount of water to their land and who keep the *levadas* clean and flowing.

As well as bringing water to farmers, the canals have proved to be ideal walkways, with a network of over 2000km winding across the island at gentle gradients. Today *levada* walking has become big business, with several tour companies offering guided *levada* walks. Though this has had the inevitable effect of removing the solitude from some of the walks, it has had the advantage of encouraging the local government to improve signposting and to provide dangerous sections of *levadas* with new fencing.

Walking tour operators

Madeira Explorers ☎291 763 701 ⊛www.Madeira-explorers.com.
MB Tours ☎291 203 950, ⊛www.mb-travel.com.
Natura Travel ☎291 775 882, ⊛www.madeirawalks.com.
Turitrans (Caniço de Baixo) ☎291 935 532, ⊛www.turitrans-infocentre.com.

Cycling and adventure sports

With its arduous gradients and narrow roads, Madeira does not lend itself to casual cycling. However, it is possible to cycle along some footpaths and *levadas*, as well as across the inland plain, Paúl da Serra.

A good way to see some of the best of the island is to take a half- or full-day organized mountain-bike tour. Tours can be arranged by Terras de Aventura (☎ 291 776 818, ⊛ www .terrasdeaventura.com); they also offer canyoning, canoeing, hang-gliding and watersports. The relatively flat island of Porto Santo is much more cycle-friendly and nearly all the main hotels rent out bikes; see p.000 for details.

Diving

Many of the larger hotels can arrange scuba diving, usually in the protected waters around Garajau and Caniço de Baixo, or off Machico. To hire equipment, you will need to show a diving certificate, logbook and sometimes a medical certificate. Basic equipment hire starts at around €25 per day. Most places also arrange four- to five-day internationally recognized PADI diving courses for beginners, for around €350–450. Once in the sea, you can swim face to face with moray eels, conger eels, squid, octopus, monkfish, tuna, parrot fish, mantas and Atlantic rays.

Diving centres

Baleia Diving Center *Hotel Dom Pedro Baia*, Machico ☎968 052 543, ⊛baleia@mail.telepac.pt.
Baleira Diving Hotel Vila Baleira, Porto Santo ☎912 240 548.
Manta Diving Center *Lido Galomar*, Caniço de Baixo ☎291 935 588, ⊛www .mantadiving.com.

Surfing and other watersports

Madeira was discovered as a **surfing** destination by intrepid Portuguese and Brazilian surfers during the 1990s, and now hosts an annual leg of the World Surfing Championships, usually in January or February in Jardim do Mar. A European surfing competition takes place in Paúl do Mar in September, though you need great expertise to participate. Madeira's deep Atlantic waters supply superb breakers, and the main attraction is the challenge of the big riders – three-metre-high waves which crash onto the basalt rock of the sea bed; extreme care and skill is required. As yet, there is no surfing association and there are no surf shops on Madeira, either, so surfers are advised to take their own board repair kits. Further information can be found on ⊛www.surfing-waves.com and ⊛www .wannasurf.com.

The Atlantic also offers ideal conditions for **windsurfing** – a native Madeiran won the 1996 World Windsurfing Championship – and many of the major hotels in Funchal rent out windsurfing equipment. Praia Formosa is a good place to try it, with equipment hire from €15 an hour. This is also the best place to hire **jet-skis** and **waterskis**; expect to pay around €50 per hour.

Boat trips, sea fishing and dolphin watching

There are countless boat trips on offer from Funchal harbour, from simple cruises to dolphin watching and fishing – you can even tour on a replica of Christopher Columbus' galleon, the Santa Maria de Colombo (☎291 220 327). Two- to three-hour trips start at around €25. Historically, Madeira had a flourishing whaling industry, but now whaling is prohibited and its waters offer a safe haven for sea mammals. **Whales** rarely go near Funchal's coastline, though they can occasionally be seen in deeper water, while **dolphins** are far more common closer to the shore. The 23-metre catamaran Sea Born (☎291 231 312, ⊛www.seaborn.pt.vu) offers dolphin watching from €25. Similar trips are offered on the yachts Ventura do Mar (☎291 280 033, ⊛www.venturadomar .com) and Gavião (☎291 241 124, ⓔ gaviaomadeira@netmadeira.com), which also runs trips to the neighbouring Ilhas Desertas.

The deep off-shore waters around the island offer some of the world's best big game **fishing**, especially for Atlantic blue marlin, which can weigh over 1000lbs (in season June–Sept). Other fish include blue eye tuna (June–Sept), blue shark, hammerhead shark, barracuda, bonito and wahoo (April–Oct), and Manta rays (Aug–Oct). Various fishing operators operate from Funchal marina.

Fishing trip operators

Katherine B Marina do Funchal, Funchal ☎291 752 685, ⊛www.fishmadeira.com. **Nautisantos** Marina do Funchal, Funchal ☎291 231 312, ⊛www.nautisantos fishing.com. **Xiphias Sport Fishing** Marina do Funchal, Funchal, ☎291 289 007 ⊛www.xiphias .no.sapo.pt.

Football

Madeira's top sides are Funchal-based Marítimo (⊛ www.maritimomadeira. com), which plays in the top Portuguese league and sometimes represents Portugal in Europe; and Nacional (⊛www .nacional-da-madeira.com), which also entertains top sides like Porto and Benfica.

Marítimo plays at the **Barreiros Stadium** on Rua do Dr Pita in Funchal (☎291 205 000), while Nacional plays in the Estádio E Rui Alves in Choupana (☎291 223 855). Tickets can be bought for most matches from the stadiums, or in advance from the club shops in Funchal (Nacional: Rua do Esmeraldo 46; Marítimo: Rua Dom Carlos 14).

Tennis

Most of the major hotels have their own tennis courts. In Funchal, there are public courts at Quinta Magnolia on Dr Pita (daily 8am–9pm; ☎291 763 237; see p.72). Courts can be booked at the main gate for just €1.75 per hour.

Golf

Madeira boasts two quality golf courses in spectacular positions: Santo da Serra (see p.131), which hosts the Madeira Open, and Palheiro Golf (see p.101). Inexperienced golfers can have lessons at either course, though only the latter allows inexperienced golfers onto the greens. If you plan to play a lot of golf, it is worth asking the clubs for the names of hotels whose guests get a discount on the fees. Porto Santo also has a highly rated nineteen-hole course and may soon be on the Portuguese Open circuit (see p.184). Details of the courses are given in the guide, or see ⊛www .Madeira-golf.com.

Children's Madeira

Recommended attractions for children include the Aqua Park at Santa Cruz (see p.118), the Parque Temático in Santana (see p.169), the aquarium in Porto Moniz (see p.156), the toboggan ride in Monte (see p.97) and the various cable cars, in Monte, Santana and Achada da Cruz.

The larger package **hotels** generally have good facilities for children, though it is worth establishing what is available

before you book. Many places have children's swimming pools, play areas and – for older kids – games rooms. Some hotels also offer babysitting and the smarter ones have creche facilities and special kids' programmes.

Most **restaurants** can offer pasta dishes and often pizzas. When cooked, *espada* can also bear more than a passing resemblance to fish and chips. All places offer a range of ice creams and desserts.

For those with babies, fresh milk – *leite do dia* – can usually only be bought from larger supermarkets. Smaller shops tend to stock only long-life milk. International-brand baby foods, nappies and baby products are all widely available in supermarkets and chemists.

Holidays and festivals

Madeira has a good share of public holidays, during which banks and most shops close and buses operate to a Sunday timetable. However, most tourist services – including most cafés, restaurants and sites – function as normal.

Madeira also has a seemingly endless supply of **festivals**, which crop up all over the island – the biggest and best of them are listed below. See also p.28.

Festivals

January
Night Festival and End of New Year Festivities (January 6). The official end of the New Year's festivities, with live music and dance in Funchal and elsewhere.
February–March
Carnival festivities in Funchal (see box on p.60).
April–May
Festa da Flor Three-day flower festival in Funchal. Main events include the Wall of Hope Ceremony, in which children pin posies onto the city hall in Funchal and make a wish, and a parade the following day.
June
Santos Populares (Popular Saints). June sees the celebration of the main saints' days:
St Anthony, the patron saint of lovers (June

13). Evening festivities include the tradition of jumping over fires (it is said that the highest leapers will be lucky in love).
St John (June 24) is the big saint's day for Funchal, with shops competing to prepare the most lavishly decorated mock altar. Evening festivities centre on Largo do Carmo.
St Peter (June 29), the patron saint of fishermen celebrated most enthusiastically in the fishing ports of Câmara de Lobos and in Ribeira Brava.
Vintage Car Rally. Some 60 vehicles dating back to the 1920s tour round the island, starting and finishing in Funchal.
July
Dança de 24 horas. Various folk dancing groups gather in Santana to perform over a riotous 24-hour period – and sometimes longer – with food and drink stalls to help keep them going.
August
Madeira Wine Rally (first weekend). International amateur rally drivers speed round the island's precipitous roads in what is considered one of most challenging rallies in Europe.
Festival of the Assumption (August 15). Island-wide celebrations. The biggest is at Nossa Senhora do Monte in Monte (August 14–15).
Festa do Santissimo Sacramento (Festival of the Holy Sacrament; last Sunday of August). A carnival-style procession departs from Machico, culminating in a huge bonfire on the neighbouring Pico de Facho.

Public holidays

1 January	5 October Republic Day
25 April Revolution Day	1 November All Saints' Day
1 May Labour Day	1 December Independence Day
10 June Portugal/Camões Day	8 December Immaculate Conception
1 July Discovery of Madeira Day	25 December
15 August Assumption	

September

Nossa Senhora da Piedade (third Sunday). A statue of the Virgin is taken from a chapel in the cliffs above Prainha to Caniçal by fishermen in a procession of boats.

Madeira Wine Festival The wine harvest is celebrated with bare-foot wine treading and folk dancing in Estreito de Câmara de Lobos, at Quinta Furão (near Santana), and with special shows and exhibitions in Funchal. There is also a Grape Festival in Porto da Cruz.

Columbus Week A week's festivities in honour of Christopher Colombus on Porto Santo (see box on p.182).

Festa de Senhor Jesus Religious festival in Ponta Delgada when a holy relic is paraded round the village (see p.163).

November

Festa das Castanhas (Chestnut Festival). Folk displays and chestnut dishes are on offer in Curral das Freiras to celebrate the local harvest.

December

Christmas Spectacular Christmas lights are turned on in Funchal on December 8. On December 16, traditional nativity scenes are set up. For locals, the main event is on December 24, with Midnight Mass followed by a traditional meal of *bacalhau*. On Christmas Day, most hotels lay on special Christmas meals and events.

New Year's Eve Funchal has a justifiable reputation as one of the best places in the world to see in the New Year. Virtually every house in the city puts on all its lights, the harbour is jammed with visiting cruise liners, and at midnight the whole bay becomes a riot of exploding fireworks and blasting ships' sirens. It is traditional to see in the new year with *bolo de mel* and champagne. Be aware that many hotels have obligatory New Year's Eve "gala" dinners at stonking rates, which can cost over €100 per person – check to see what you're tied to before you book.

Directory

Addresses In the larger towns, addresses in Madeira follow the Portuguese convention of having the street name followed by the building number. A house or building number followed by, for example, 4° shows it is on the fourth floor. However, in smaller villages the address may simply consist of the name of the house, café or hotel without any street name, or with a general area name such as *Sítio da Igreja*, roughly meaning "in the place where the church is".

Airlines TAP Air Portugal, Avda do Mar 10 and airport (☎291 520 821); British Airways, airport (☎291 520 870); GB Airways, airport (☎291 524 539); Portugália (airport ☎291 524 510).

Airport information ☎291 220 064 (Madeira); ☎291 980 120 (Porto Santo).

Clothes Though Madeira is warm all year, take a warm top for the cooler evenings and for visiting the mountains. A light raincoat is also recommended year-round.

Consulates Britain, Av Zarco 2–4, Funchal ☎291 221 221; USA, Ed. Infante, Bloco B, AP. B-4, Funchal ☎291 235 636.

Electricity The current is 220 volts AC. Most sockets take two-point round pins as in continental Europe. UK appliances work with an adaptor, but North American appliances will also need a transformer.

Emergencies Call ☎112 for police, ambulance or fire brigade.

Gay scene Most of the island has a conservative attitude to homosexuality, though in Funchal people are more open-minded. Its annual carnival kicks off with a transvestite night, and though there are no specific bars or clubs for gays, *Café do Teatro* (see p.65) is a popular gay hangout.

Hospital Hospital Cruz Carvalho, Av Luís Camões, Funchal (☎291 705 600). Most villages – and Porto Santo – also have a Centro da Saúde (health centre) for basic care.

Lost property Rua Infância 28 ☎291 208 400, or the airport ☎291 524 913.

Pharmacy For minor health complaints you should go to a *farmácia* (pharmacy), which you'll find in almost any village. Most have someone who can speak English. The pharmacists are trained to dispense suitable medication that would normally only be available on prescription in Britain or North America. Pharmacies are usually open Mon–Fri 9am–1pm & 3–7pm; Sat 9am–1pm. In the larger towns, they take it in turns to stay open out-of-hours (*fora das horas*); check in any pharmacy window for the address of the one which is open.

Phones Nearly all hotels have their own telephones, but these are invariably more expensive than public phones. It is best to make international calls using a *credifone*, a phone card which you can buy in denominations of €3, €6 or €9 from post offices, some newspaper kiosks and shops with a CTT sign. The main post offices also have pay cabins charging the same rate as a *credifone*; take a token from the attendant and pay for the call at the end. The cheap rate for international calls is between 10pm and 8am and at weekends. Most UK, Australian and New Zealand Mobile phones will work in Madeira, though US-bought handsets, which use a different system, may not. Check with your phone provider.

Photography For digital or conventional film processing, try Foto Continental, Gal. São Lourenço loja 27, Av Arriaga 8 or Belafoto, with a branch the Anadia Shopping centre on Rua Visconde Anadia just up from the main market.

Police To report a theft or any crime, go to the main station on Rua Infância 28 ☎291 208 400. On Porto Santo, the main police station is at Sítio das Matas in Vila Baleira ☎291 982 423.

Post office Funchal's main post office is on Avenida Calouste Gulbenkian 3, next to the SAM bus terminal (Mon–Fri 8.30am–6.30pm). The city's most central post office is on Avenida Zarco (Mon–Fri 8.30am–8pm, Sat 9am–1pm). The main post office in Porto Santo is on Avenida Vieira de Castro, Vila Baleira, opposite the tourist office (Mon–Fri 9am–6pm, Sat 9am–1pm).

Shopping Traditional shopping hours are Monday to Friday 9am–1pm & 3–7pm, Saturday 9am–1pm. Some shopping centres and tourist shops stay open for lunch and until 10pm Monday to Saturday.

Supermarkets Madeira's biggest and best supermarket is Pingo Doce. There are several branches round the town, such as opposite the Lido and at Anadia Shopping on Rua Visconde Anadia just up from the main market (open daily 9am–10pm). There are also branches in Machico, on Rua General António Teixeira de Aguiar and Vila Baleira on Porto Santo, on the junction of Av Dr Manuel Gregório Pestana Júnior and Rua Bartolomeu Perestrelo.

Time Madeira follows GMT (late Sept to late March) and BST (late March to late Oct). This is 5hr ahead of Eastern Standard Time and 8hr ahead of Pacific Standard Time.

Tipping As on the Portuguese mainland, large tips are not expected. Service charges are normally included in hotel and restaurant bills. If you are particularly pleased with the service of a porter, maid or waiter, leave ten percent of the bill.

Toilets There are public toilets in most towns. You should tip attendants.

Water is safe to drink from a tap anywhere on the island, though on neighbouring Porto Santo it is best to stick to bottled water: as the tap water is desalinated, it tastes revolting. In theory, water in *levadas* is also safe to drink on the higher mountain slopes, but should definitely not be drunk lower down as it may have passed through farm land.

Language

Portuguese

English is widely spoken in the majority of Madeira's hotels and tourist restaurants, but you will find a few words of Portuguese extremely useful if you are travelling on public transport, or in more out-of-the-way places. If you have some knowledge of Spanish, you won't have much problem reading Portuguese. Understanding it when it's spoken, though, is a another matter: pronunciation is entirely different and at first even the easiest words are hard to distinguish. Once you've started to figure out how words are pronounced it gets a lot easier very quickly.

A useful word is **há** (the H is silent), which means "there is" or "is there?" and can be used for just about anything. Thus: "*Há uma pensão aqui?*" (Is there a guesthouse here?) More polite and better in shops or restaurants are "**Tem**…?" (pronounced *taying*) which means "Do you have…?", or "**Queria**…" (I'd like…). And of course there are the old standards "Do you speak English?" (*Fala Inglês?*) and "I don't understand" (*Não compreendo*).

Pronunciation

The chief difficulty with **pronunciation** is its lack of clarity – consonants tend to be slurred, vowels nasal and often ignored altogether. The **consonants** are, at least, consistent:

C is soft before E and I, hard otherwise unless it has a cedilla – *açucar* (sugar) is pronounced "assookar".

CH is somewhat softer than in English; *chá* (tea) sounds like Shah.

J is pronounced like the "s" in pleasure, as is G except when it comes before a "hard" vowel (A, O and U).

LH sounds like "lyuh" – *pilha* (battery) is pronounced "pillya".

Q is always pronounced as a "k".

S before a consonant or at the end of a word becomes "sh", otherwise it's as in English – Sagres (the beer) is pronounced "Sahgresh".

X is also pronounced "sh"– *caixa* (cash desk) is pronounced "kaisha".

Vowels are worse – flat and truncated, they're often difficult for English-speaking tongues to get around. The only way to learn is to listen: accents, **Ã**, **Ô** or **É**, turn them into longer, more familiar sounds.

When two vowels come together they continue to be enunciated separately except in the case of **EI** and **OU** – which sound like "a" and long "o" respectively. E at the end of a word is silent unless it has an accent, so that *carne* (meat) is pronounced "karn", while *café* sounds much as you'd expect. The **tilde over Ã or Õ** renders the pronunciation much like the French -an and -on endings only more nasal. More common is **ÃO** (as in *pão*, bread; *são*, saint; *limão*, lemon), which sounds something like a strangled yelp of "Ow!" cut off in midstream.

Words and phrases

Essentials

sim; não	yes; no
olá; bom dia	hello; good morning
boa tarde/noite	good afternoon/ night
adeus, até logo	goodbye, see you later
hoje; amanhã	today; tomorrow
por favor/se faz favor	please
tudo bem?	is everything all right?
está bem	it's all right/OK
obrigado/a*	thank you
onde; que	where; what
quando; porquê	when; why
como; quanto	how; how much
não sei	I don't know
sabe ...?	do you know ...?
pode ...?	could you ...?
desculpe; com licença	sorry; excuse me
este/a; esse/a	this; that
agora; mais tarde	now; later
mais; menos	more; less
grande; pequeno	big; little
aberto; fechado	open; closed
senhoras; homens	women; men
lavabo/quarto de banho	toilet/bathroom

*Obrigado agrees with the sex of the person speaking – a woman says obrigada, a man obrigado.

Getting around

esquerda, direita, sempre em frente	left, right, straight ahead
aqui; ali	here; there
perto; longe	near; far
Onde é a estação de camionetas?	Where is the bus station?
a paragem de autocarro para ...	the bus stop for ...
Donde parte o autocarro para ...?	Where does the bus to ... leave from?
A que horas parte?	What time does it leave?
(chega a ...?)	(arrive at ...?)
Pare aqui por favor	Stop here please
um bilhete (para)	a ticket (to)
ida e volta	round trip

Accommodation

Queria um quarto	I'd like a room
É para uma noite (semana)	It's for one night (week)
É para uma pessoa (duas pessoas)	It's for one person (two people)
Quanto custa?	How much is it?
Posso ver?	May I see/look around?
Há um quarto mais barato?	Is there a cheaper room?/
com uma vista	with a view (of the sea)?
com duche?	with a shower?

Shopping

Quanto é?	How much is it?
banco; câmbio	bank; change
correios	post office
(dois) selos	(two) stamps
Como se diz isto em Português?	What's this called in Portuguese?
O que é isso?	What's that?

Days of the week

domingo	Sunday
segunda-feira	Monday
terça-feira	Tuesday
quarta-feira	Wednesday
quinta-feira	Thursday
sexta-feira	Friday
sábado	Saturday

Numbers

1	um
2	dois
3	três
4	quatro
5	cinco
6	seis
7	sete
8	oito
9	nove
10	dez
11	onze
12	doze
13	treze
14	catorze
15	quinze
16	dezasseis
17	dezassete
18	dezoito
19	dezanove
20	vinte
21	vinte e um
30	trinta
40	quarenta
50	cinquenta
60	sessenta
70	setenta
80	oitenta
90	noventa
100	cem
101	cento e um
200	duzentos
500	quinhentos
1000	mil

Common Portuguese signs

Ar condicionado	air conditioned
Desvio	diversion (on road)
Dormidas	private rooms
Elevador	lift
Entrada	entrance
Fecha a porta	close the door
Incluído IVA	(price) includes VAT
Obras	roadworks
Paragem	bus stop
Perigo/Perigoso	danger/dangerous
Pré-pagamento	pay in advance
Proibido estacionar	no parking
Quartos	private rooms
Saída	exit
Turismo	tourist office

Menu glossary

Starters, staples and side dishes

arroz	rice
azeitonas	olives
batatas fritas	chips
batatas cozidas	boiled potatoes
canja	chicken broth
legumes	vegetables
manteiga	butter
ovo cozido	boiled egg
pão	bread
pimenta	pepper
piri-piri	chilli sauce
presunto	smoked ham
queijo	cheese
sal	salt
salada (mista)	(mixed) salad
sopa	soup
sopa de peixe/ legumes/tomate	fish/vegetable/ tomato soup

Meat

borrego	lamb
carne de porco	pork
carne de vaca	beef
costeletas de porco	pork chops
dobrada/tripas	tripe
febras	pork steaks
fígado	liver
frango	young chicken
galinha	chicken
vitela	veal

Fish and seafood

atum	tuna
bodião	parrot fish
camarões	shrimps
caranguejo	crab
carapau	mackerel
chocos	cuttle fish

espadarte	swordfish
gambas	prawns
lagosta	lobster
lapas	limpets
linguada	sole
lulas	squid
pargo	sea bream
pescada	hake
polvo	octopus
salmão	salmon
salmonete	red mullet
sardinhas	sardines
truta	trout

Portuguese and Madeiran specialities

bacalhau à brás	salted cod with egg and potatoes
caldeirada	fish stew
cataplana	fish, shellfish or meat stewed in a circular metal dish
espada com banana /vinho e alhos	scabbard fish with banana/ wine and garlic
espetada	kebab, usually beef
feijoada	bean casserole
milho frito	fried cornmeal
pão com alho	garlic bread

Desserts (Sobremesa)

gelado	ice cream
melão	melon
morangos	strawberries
pudim flan	crème caramel
salada da fruta	fruit salad
uvas	grapes

Other useful terms

almoço	lunch
cadeira	chair
colher	spoon
conta	the bill
copo	glass
ementa	menu
faca	knife
garfo	fork
jantar	dinner
mesa	table
quanto é?	how much is it?

quarto de banho	toilet
queria...	I'd like...
pequeno almoco	breakfast
pimenta	pepper
sal	salt

Cakes and snacks

bolos	cakes
bolo de mel	"honey cake" made of dried fruits, spices and molasses
pastéis de bacalhau	salted cod rissoles
pastéis de nata	custard-cream tarts
prego	garlic beef in a roll
rissois de camarão	fried shrimp puffs
sandes	sandwich
sandes de fiambre/ queijo	ham/cheese sandwich

Coffee, tea and soft drinks

água (sem/com gás)	mineral water (without/with gas)
brisa maracujá	fizzy passion fruit juice
sumo de laranja/ maçã	orange/apple juice
chá	tea
café	coffee
sem/com leite	without/with milk
sem/com açúcar	without/with sugar
uma bica	a small, strong espresso

Alcoholic drinks

um copo/uma garrafa de/da	a glass/bottle of ...
aguardente	firewater distilled from sugar cane
licor de castanha	a distillation of the local chestnuts
poncha aguardente	mixed with brandy, lemon and honey
sidra	cider
vinho branco/tinto	white/red wine
cerveja	beer
um imperial	a half glass
uma caneca	a large glass (half-litre)

ROUGH GUIDES TRAVEL...

Rough Guides are available from good bookstores worldwide. New titles are
published every month. Check www.roughguides.com for the latest news.

...MUSIC & REFERENCE

Also! More than 120 Rough Guide music CDs are available from all good book and record stores. Listen in at www.worldmusic.net

Quinta Mãe dos Homens
Funchal...

...your room with a view!

Quinta Mãe dos Homens offers spectacular views
of the Bay of Funchal and beyond.
Concealed within the Quinta's 8 acre grounds
lie 24 self catering Studio's, one bedroom
apartments and family Villa's all with private
terraces or balconies. Along with the Clubhouse
and it's terrace overlooking the swimming pool
make it Funchal's number one self catering holiday!

Visit our web site at www.qmdh.com
For further information please contact reservations on:
00 351 291 204410 or e-mail. quinta.mdh@netmadeira.com

small print & Index

A Rough Guide to Rough Guides

Madeira DIRECTIONS is published by Rough Guides. The first *Rough Guide to Greece*, published in 1982, was a student scheme that became a publishing phenomenon. The immediate success of the book – with numerous reprints and a Thomas Cook prize short-listing – spawned a series that rapidly covered dozens of destinations. Rough Guides had a ready market among low-budget backpackers, but soon also acquired a much broader and older readership that relished Rough Guides' wit and inquisitiveness as much as their enthusiastic, critical approach. Everyone wants value for money, but not at any price. Rough Guides soon began supplementing the "rougher" information about hostels and low-budget listings with the kind of detail on restaurants and quality hotels that independent-minded visitors on any budget might expect, whether on business in New York or trekking in Thailand. These days the guides offer recommendations from shoestring to luxury and cover a large number of destinations around the globe, including almost every country in the Americas and Europe, more than half of Africa and most of Asia and Australasia. Rough Guides now publish:

• Travel guides to more than 200 worldwide destinations
• Dictionary phrasebooks to 22 major languages
• Maps printed on rip-proof and waterproof Polyart™ paper
• Music guides running the gamut from Opera to Elvis
• Reference books on topics as diverse as the Weather and Shakespeare
• World Music CDs in association with World Music Network

Publishing information

This 1st edition published October 2005 by **Rough Guides Ltd**, 80 Strand, London WC2R 0RL. 345 Hudson St, 4th Floor, New York, NY 10014, USA.

Distributed by the Penguin Group
Penguin Books Ltd, 80 Strand, London WC2R 0RL
Penguin Group (USA), 375 Hudson Street, NY 10014, USA
Penguin Group (Australia), 250 Camberwell Road, Camberwell, Victoria 3124, Australia
Penguin Group (Canada), 10 Alcorn Avenue, Toronto, ON M4V 1E4, Canada
Penguin Group (New Zealand), Cnr Rosedale and Airborne Roads, Albany, Auckland, New Zealand
Typeset in Bembo and Helvetica to an original design by Henry Iles.
Printed and bound in China

© Matthew Hancock 2005

224pp includes index

A catalogue record for this book is available from the British Library

ISBN 1-84353-446-0

The publishers and authors have done their best to ensure the accuracy and currency of all the information in **Madeira DIRECTIONS**, however, they can accept no responsibility for any loss, injury, or inconvenience sustained by any traveller as a result of information or advice contained in the guide.

1 3 5 7 9 8 6 4 2

Help us update

We've gone to a lot of effort to ensure that the first edition of **Madeira DIRECTIONS** is accurate and up to date. However, things change – places get "discovered", opening hours are notoriously fickle, restaurants and rooms raise prices or lower standards. If you feel we've got it wrong or left something out, we'd like to know, and if you can remember the address, the price, the phone number, so much the better.

We'll credit all contributions, and send a copy of the next edition (or any other DIRECTIONS guide or Rough Guide if you prefer) for the best letters. Everyone who writes to us and isn't already a subscriber will receive a copy of our full-colour thrice-yearly newsletter. Please mark letters: "**Madeira DIRECTIONS Update**" and send to: Rough Guides, 80 Strand, London WC2R 0RL, or Rough Guides, 4th Floor, 345 Hudson St, New York, NY 10014. Or send an email to **mail@roughguides.com**

Have your questions answered and tell others about your trip at **www.roughguides.atinfopop.**

Rough Guide credits

Text editor: Ruth Blackmore
Layout: Diana Jarvis
Photography: Helena Smith
Cartography: Rajesh Mishra
Picture editor: Harriet Mills

Proofreader: Susannah Wight
Production: Katherine Owers
Design: Henry Iles
Cover design: Chloë Roberts

SMALL PRINT

The author

Freelance writer Matthew Hancock commutes regularly to Portugal and likes nothing better than putting on his boots to walk Madeira's *levadas*.

Now resident in Dorset, he is also author of *Algarve* and *Lisbon* Directions and co-author of the *Rough Guide to Portugal*.

Acknowledgements

The author would like to thank all the people who helped with the guide, especially Jane Gordon, Teresa Ventura, Maria Luisa Perestrello and Idalino. Also to Isabel Branco, Isabel Ferraz, Katja Hekkala, António Correia, Pauline Engelse and *Reid's Palace*

Hotel, and to the usual support from Amanda Tomlin. At Rough Guides thanks to Ruth Blackmore for patient editing, Helena Smith for superb photos, Harriet Mills for picture editing, Diana Jarvis for typesetting and Rajesh Mishra for maps.

Photo credits

All images © Rough Guides except the following:

Front cover picture: View from Quinta Furão © Helena Smith

Back cover picture: Ponta do Rosto © Alamy
Colour photos
p.7 DragonTree © Matthew Hancock
p.8 Porto Santo beach umbrellas © Matthew Hancock
p.11 Pico Ruivo © Matthew Hancock
p.11 Porto Santo beach © Matthew Hancock
p.12 Lorano to Machico walk © Matthew Hancock
p.14 Lift to Fajã das Padres © Matthew Hancock
p.15 Cable car at Santana © Matthew Hancock
p.15 Santa Maria de Columbus © Matthew Hancock
p.16 Diving © Madeira Tourism
p.16 Porto Santo golf course © Matthew Hancock
p.17 2004 UEFA Cup, Maritmo vs. Glasgow Rangers © Duarte Sa/Reuters/Corbis
p.17 Mountain biking © Madeira Tourism
p.17 Surfing © Madeira Tourism
p.18 Portela plant stalls © Matthew Hancock
p.20 Porto Santo beach © Matthew Hancock
p.21 Prainha beach © Matthew Hancock
p.21 Porto da Cruz pool © Madeira Tourism
p.24 Museu de Arte Sacra © Madeira Tourism
p.25 Casa Museu Cristovão Colombo © Madeira Tourism
p.25 Museu Photografia Vicentes © www.madeiraonline.com
p.28 Carros antigos vintage car © Madeira Tourism
p.28 Grape treading at wine festival, Câmara de Lobos © Prisma Die-Agentur/Powerstock
p.29 New Year's Eve fireworks, Funchal © Helena Smith
p.29 Funchal Carnival © Madeira Tourism
p.29 Columbus Festival © Madeira Tourism
p.29 Festa da Flor, Funchal © Madeira Tourism

p.31 Funchal balloon © Matthew Hancock
p.35 Lauraceous forests © Matthew Hancock
p.35 Sir Winston Churchill and Lady Clementine at *Reid's* © *Reid's Hotel*
p.37 Porto da Cruz © Matthew Hancock
p.40 *The Cliff Bay* © Madeira Tourism
p.41 The *Armada Restaurant, Royal Savoy Hotel* © Royal Savoy Hotel
p.41 *Luamar Hotel* swimming pool © Matthew Hancock
p.43 Porto Santo Golf clubhouse © Matthew Hancock
Black and white photos
p.52 Funchal view © Matthew Hancock
p.59 Museu de Arte Sacra © www.madeira-web.com
p.64 Taxi drivers © Matthew Hancock
p.72 Pawpaw plant, Quinta Magnolia © DK Images
p.106 Fishermen playing cards, Câmara de Lobos © Matthew Hancock
p.110 Fajã dos Padres © Matthew Hancock
p.114 Diving off Caniço de Baixo © Madeira Tourism
p.116 Wicker worker, Camacha © DK Images/Linda Whitwam
p.121 Machico beachfront © Matthew Hancock
p.122 Garajao picnic spot © Matthew Hancock
p.128 Whale museum interior © Madeira Tourism
p.131 Santo Serra golf course © Madeira Tourism
p.142 Calheta, aerial view © Madeira Tourism
p.171 Homem em Pé stones © Madeira Tourism
p.173 Penha da Águia © Matthew Hancock
p.181 Town hall, Vila Baleira © Matthew Hancock
p.184 Porto Santo beach © Madeira Tourism
p.184 Porto Santo beach © Matthew Hancock
p.185 Cannon, Pico do Castelo © Matthew Hancock
p.188 Traditional windmill © Matthew Hancock

Index

Maps are marked in colour